Get Some Guts, Coach!

Jill Jackson

outskirtspress

DENVER, COLORADO

*To my mom and dad who always encouraged me to be gutsy.
I owe all good things in my life to you. I love you.*

Table of Contents

Get Some Guts

Talent is helpful…but guts are absolutely necessary.
~Jessamyn West

Coaching is the number one, most readily-available tool that has the real-life power to transform the quality of teaching and the impact of teaching on student performance. That is the one idea that I hope you understand after reading this book. We don't have to get fancy, we don't need more technology, we don't need to have another study group, we don't need to spend a zillion more hours in the training rooms. But, we do have to get focused, timely feedback into the hands of teachers so that they can immediately adjust their teaching, allowing students to learn faster, master more material and become more skilled.

It's really that simple. Coaching is about the teachers…and the kids.

The purpose of this book is to take any teacher leader, department chair, instructional coach, literacy or math coach, facilitator, mentor or peer coach and help them work with teachers to do two things:

- Reflect upon the impact of their teaching practice and,

- Refine their teaching skills so that they can increase that impact

When I facilitate coaching workshops, the organizer will often ask me to describe my philosophy of coaching so that they can include this information in the program or introduction. What I tell them is this: I don't have a philosophy on coaching, because what I bring to coaches is a series of skills that they must master in order to get into the classrooms with the teachers and get the coaching job done.

I find that oftentimes coaches get stuck on a specific philosophy of coaching and they are just that: stuck! Some have been trained to never give teachers direct advice because it might sound evaluative. My thought is that if we never give direct advice or direction, then how on earth are teachers supposed to know what they should do? Some have been trained to give three "glows" to one "grow," essentially buttering up the teachers before lowering the boom of what they need to change. I hate to break it to you, but teachers know the formula and it seems too predictable when we operate so rigidly. Some coaches have been trained to wait until the teacher comes to them for support. Well, I will say this: If you're waiting for some people who really need coaching to show up at your door, you'd better get a bowl of popcorn, a blanket, and a Netflix subscription because you'll be waiting awhile!

I know that coaching is first and foremost about relationship, second about skill, and third about results. And if we focus on much more than those things, then I think we're way off track.

Bottom line? Coaching must be about observable improvement in teacher skill if we expect it to have an impact on student achievement.

The problem is, however, that coaching real-life teachers in their natural habitat of the classroom is a challenge in so many ways! Coaching is personal and people can get easily testy, frustrated or offended. Even the most well-meaning, skilled coach can become skittish when she thinks about giving feedback to a hesitant teacher.

So what's the antidote to potentially testy, frustrated or easily-offended folks?

Guts.

Yep. It takes courage and conviction to stick with a teacher when things aren't going well or there is tension in a conversation. It takes guts to forge a relationship with teachers and get to the heart of their teaching.

Without guts, coaches end up short-selling the content, apologizing for decisions that school leadership has made, unintentionally undermining important instructional decisions, and spending too much time focusing on things that are out of the teacher's control. Without guts, the coaching power is diluted and teacher/coach trust issues start to crop up. I know that this is contrary to what you might naturally think, but I will show you how guts are absolutely essential to your success as a coach and your teachers' success in the classroom.

The good news is that you can increase your coaching power starting right now. You don't need anything new, you just need to recommit to providing your teachers the support that really gets results. And in doing so, you leave the rest of the junk behind! If there are teachers on your campus, then you have a need for coaching and you have an opportunity to improve the quality of the teaching.

Now, you may be thinking, some people call coaches by different names: instructional coaches, literacy coaches, reading coaches and instructional facilitators. From this point on, I will refer to anyone who is tasked with supporting teachers as they teach students, as "coach." The fads, philosophies, rigid approaches and labels may come and go, but the bottom line is coaches are the ones who provide support to teachers directly in the classrooms in order to improve performance of both teachers and students.

So…let's get started, Coach!

First off, I'd like for us to get really comfortable with the following idea, as it is a theme throughout the book and also a theme throughout the most successful coaching practices: *Coaching exists to increase the quality of the teaching to the extent that it will positively impact and increase the performance of the students.* If we make coaching about something more than that, we are missing the mark. We have an overwhelming amount of information from decades of school data and what seems like zillions of research studies that supports the idea that quality instruction is the most important factor in student success.

Plain and simply put: teaching matters!

Gut Check!

Take an honest assessment of your current coaching work. As an outside observer, would I say that your coaching feedback is 100 percent focused on the quality of the instruction? Eighty percent focused on the quality of the instruction? Less than 50 percent focused on the quality of the instruction?

Before we dig further into the nitty-gritty of the coaching role, we need to establish what the term "quality instruction" really means. This is the meat of coaching, the fundamentals of the coaching role.

There are two main components that underpin quality instruction: the context and the content. The context is the 'how' of teaching and the content is the 'what' of teaching.

When you look at the context of quality instruction, you see that it has two components: classroom management and student engagement. Both management and engagement are totally and completely required in order for students to master the content of any lesson. Without the context in place, you're just "teaching the lesson" with no focus on how well students are learning or engaging with the content. It is not uncommon to overhear two teachers having a conversation in the staff room in which one teacher laments, "I taught that, I just don't know why they didn't pass the test!" This is a sign that, perhaps, the teacher taught the content, but didn't plan to monitor behaviors and engage the students. Let's be clear, the teacher is responsible for engaging students – if we leave whether or not to engage up to the students, we are in deep trouble!

When teachers have a solid behavioral and classroom management system in place and they expect that students will follow that system, they get more teaching done and more content taught. Why? Because high levels of classroom management are directly related to a teacher's ability to instruct at a swift pace. Now, I'm not saying that because a teacher has a good management system, that they are automatically engaging their students at a high level, but what I am saying is that it is necessary for teachers to have a solid management system in order for content to be learned in their classrooms. There is no shortcut to management.

Once a management system is in place, the teacher must then work on engaging students in responding to and relating to the content. There are several ways to know if students are engaged: they are saying something about the content, they are writing something about the content, and/or they are doing something physical in response to the content (raising a hand to vote for a concept or giving a thumbs-up, thumbs-down response to a question, for example).

Without ways to measure (verbal, written or physical) engagement, we can mistake engagement for kids sitting really quietly. In fact, we have quite a few teachers who believe that engagement equals sustained, silent staring. And I'm here to set the record straight: if you want to know whether kids are engaged, you can only determine their engagement levels by the actions they are taking. There is no way to measure engagement when kids are sitting quietly!

In fact, we know that the more engagement we have, the fewer behavior problems we see. And the fewer behavior problems we see, the more time we have to teach the content. And the more time we have to teach, model, practice and apply the content, the more students will master.

Yes! That issue of "not enough time to teach my grade level standards" goes away when we get a handle on the classroom management and engagement. And to think, all of this before we've even talked about the content itself! In fact, so often I will see well-meaning coaches skip over the very obvious need for coaching on classroom management with a teacher because they're so focused on getting to Standard 5.9! When this happens, oftentimes the teacher and coach have to double back and fix management and engagement issues in the end, wasting coaching and preparation time. Focusing on context first allows the coach and teacher to clear the debris to make way for efficient and effective instruction.

Now let's move onto the "what" of quality teaching: the instruction and the content. Delivery of instruction and preparation and planning are the two components of improving the quality of teaching. I have had the opportunity to coach thousands of instructional coaches in prioritizing their efforts so that they can have the biggest impact. Besides forgetting to coach classroom management first, I see a second common error: coaches jumping right into what the lesson looks like when the teacher is teaching the kids.

What coaches are missing is this: without a high focus on preparation and planning, we are always going to be doubling back and trying to fix a preparation problem. Preventive coaching is a much more efficient and effective practice for teachers and their kids. We must put our instructional focus at the point of lesson inception: the teacher's plan book, as most lessons are made or broken during the planning and preparation time. I want us to make a distinction between planning and preparation that I believe to be very important: planning is figuring out what we're going to teach. Preparation is figuring how we're going to teach it.

I find that we are pretty darn good at getting the "what" in the plan book (For example, in Monday's plan box I write something like: Teach "We, the People," pg. 74), but when it comes down to really thinking through how I'm going to get kids engaged in that content, what questions I'll use to get them discussing it, what kinds of responses I want them to have during the discussion, how I'll scaffold for my English Language Learners, pre-teaching parts that are particularly difficult, and who will partner best together…well, I see a lot of that as an afterthought.

The lesson is made in its preparation phase. And boy, we are missing a huge opportunity if we fail to coach teachers in how to prepare their lessons.

I was recently working with a group of middle school teachers on designing lessons that are Common Core aligned and one teacher said, "Oh, I love it when I have a teachable moment…I love it when a student says something that really sparks my ideas and we got off in a direction that I didn't even see coming! That's the best part of teaching!" I disagree. What concerns me about teachable moments is that they are wholly and entirely based upon the students' bringing up that particular topic or idea. It's not planned for. If a student doesn't spark that particular teachable moment for the teacher, then the kids in that class don't get that instruction. And that's a problem!

Instead, what we need to do is make sure that our coaching efforts are focused on how to create lesson plans that ensure that the teachable moments will happen for all kids – everyday and on cue. Once we've orchestrated the structure of the lesson, then the next coaching focus can be on how efficiently and effectively that instruction is actually taught to the real-life kids.

The "A-Ha moment" that I hope you're having as you read this is: *I've got a whole lot of work to do as I coach teachers before I should begin working on the actual delivery of the lesson. In fact, if I focus only on delivery (and avoid classroom management, engagement and lesson preparation and planning), I might be treating a symptom, not the deep rooted area in need of coaching. I am my most powerful as a Coach when I am working at the very heart of what constitutes quality instruction.*

While you may have been hired as coach to work on a particular initiative or focus area, each and every coach must start here, in this order:

1. Classroom management

2. Student engagement

3. Lesson preparation and planning

4. Delivery of instruction

Of course some teachers will be working at the classroom management level for months while others are at the lesson preparation level, but everyone moves through these four areas.

When I hear leaders, coaches and teachers say, "Oh it would be much better if the coach could just be in the classrooms pulling groups of struggling kids," I realize that there is naiveté about the impact that coaching can have – this is short-sighted thinking. Of course, it would be great to have a coach in your classroom pulling your five lowest performers – I mean, he can get them out of your hair for a bit! It really seems like having another adult in the classroom, allowing you to lower your group size for a half-hour a day seems like a good idea, but most often that's just another "symptom" fix. Lowering the class size doesn't mean that the management, engagement, preparation and delivery is going to improve. In fact, I've seen very well behaved and engaged classes of forty, and very poorly behaved and disengaged groups of three!

Management, engagement, preparation, planning and delivery are what matter in getting students to master any type of new content across all content areas. And in order to be effective, coaching must be organized around them.

Gut Check!

I want you to stop for a second, right now, and just do a quick reflection on how and where you've been spending your coaching time – use these questions to help guide you:

- Have you done a walk-through check of classroom management in every classroom?

- Have you modeled classroom management and behavior techniques for teachers struggling with classroom management?

- Are you working on instruction with some teachers when you should be working on their management of the classroom?

- When did you last spend time supporting a teacher during his lesson prep?

- Which teachers do you need to provide engagement support to?

- Which classrooms could become models on your campus for preparation, management, engagement and overall stellar delivery?

Your responses to the questions in the Gut Check above will help you take an honest look at what the content of your coaching is. Here's the big idea: the quality, content and context of your coaching matters, just as they matter for teachers!

In later chapters, we will look at how to improve both the content and context of your coaching, but for now we have to look at what types of coaching activities have the biggest impact on the quality of teaching.

There is so much research and data that supports the notion that our current forms of professional development (the "sit and get" style that we're so used to) are lacking in their impact on teachers and students. I often say, if the amount of professional development equaled the level of student achievement, companies like mine wouldn't even exist. After all, what we see again and again is that teachers aren't lacking in professional development or training, they're struggling to get the training content into regular practice in their classrooms.

The research on coaching is very clear: *true impact on quality instructional practice comes through a combination of research, training, modeling, feedback and, most importantly, coaching.* Coaching is the relationship-driven focus on the technical aspects of the instructional "give-and-take" between the teacher and the students.

There are many ways to spend coaching time:

- Spending hours tracking and plotting data

- On-the-fly subbing in small groups when the teacher or instructional aide is absent

- Supporting teachers with their managerial tasks

- Working only with certain teachers who ask for help

- Chronically attending professional development meetings or seminars

- Bar coding the latest shipment of instructional materials

- Spending hours working on the instructional schedule

But what we know is that if we are spending time on crunching the data, instead of spending time with the teachers in their classrooms, the quality of instruction will suffer. If we gather every material and run every copy of a master that teachers might need, the quality of teaching will suffer. If we decide to "pull kids" to a small group as a band-aid to interventions, the quality of teaching will suffer. And if we beat around the bush and deliver feedback and information to a small group of teachers instead of one-on-one to teachers in real time, the quality of teaching will suffer. While none of these coaching activities is negative or bad, the sum of these does not equal the impact on student achievement that working one-on-one with a teacher can have.

Now I must say, I've never caught a coach sitting around getting her nails done or with her feet up eating bonbons (although that's what some teachers think coaches do, don't they?). In fact, there are many coaches that I have known who are wildly busy! They are just wildly busy on things that don't relate to the quality of teaching.

Is that you?

It is essential to recommit to what coaching is and what it isn't, and align our work to what's happening smack-dab in the classrooms every day. Consider this as you align yourself to what really gets coaching results:

Coaching is…	Coaching isn't…
▪ Individualized to each teacher	▪ Optional
▪ Improving the quality of instruction	▪ Punitive
▪ Improving the effect of the instruction on student performance	▪ Personal
▪ Professional development	▪ Tattling to the administrator
▪ Diagnosing teacher needs, based upon student data	▪ Unlimited patience
▪ Focusing on specific teaching skills	▪ Always comfortable
▪ Intentional	▪ Paperwork based
▪ Inspiring, motivational	▪ Fly-by-the-seat-of-my-pants
▪ Face-to-face	▪ Subbing in the classrooms
▪ Communicating care and serving as an example to teachers	▪ By teacher invitation only
▪ Providing positive feedback	▪ Working with kids directly
▪ Providing corrective feedback	▪ Doing work for teachers
▪ Modeling	▪ Acting as the go-between the leader and teacher
▪ In the classroom	

I know this to be true: *there is no coaching activity or task completed that will trump the return on investment of getting into a classroom and supporting a teacher before, during and after instruction.*

Many coaches spend way too much planning time, collaboration time, professional development time, and leadership and coaching time merely *talking* about things teachers should do. Very little, if any, actual in-classroom coaching is taking place – and that is why the return on investment of professional development is so low. We have ignored the data that tells us that coaching is the number one tool for getting training information into practice. And without getting that training information into practice in the classrooms, there is literally no way that the training we provide teachers will impact student achievement.

Gut Check!

Just take a second and reflect on these questions:

- If I were to poll my staff and ask them what the definition of coaching is, does it match the "Coaching Is/ Coaching Isn't" chart?

- Where have I gotten off track and where am I right on target with my coaching?

- Do I need to schedule time with my principal to calibrate (or recalibrate) our vision of what coaching should look like in our school?

- What areas do I need to hit the "reset" button on so that, from here on out, I can increase the power and impact of my coaching?

Coaching is the very intersection of the content, the teaching and the students. We need to get candid about coaching focus and coaching activities to ensure that the return on the professional development time is what it could be. The good news? If you're a bit out of focus on your coaching work, you can turn it around quickly.

That's why I wrote this book.

Connect Your Coaching to the Common Core

The implementation of the Common Core is giving all of us a level playing field because it's brand new to everyone! Take advantage of this and start to study the Standards systematically. Here's how:

Analyze the Standards and determine their level of complexity by correlating the verbs in the Standards to Webb's Depth of Knowledge

Read Appendix B of the Standards document on CoreStandards.org

Go to the PARCC and Smarter Balanced websites and scout out the released items. And if you're feeling incredibly brave, take the online practice tests!

Coaching Through Those Sticky Situations

Facebook fan, Robin H. asks: *How do you move people past the myth of coaches being only for struggling teachers?*

What an important question, Robin. Boy, we have a lot of coaches who are experiencing this very thought! Here are some ways I typically handle the "coaches are for losers only" mentality:

1. I re-establish with the principal the importance of using coaching as a vehicle or tool for evaluation. Now before you freak out, let me explain! (Coaching and evaluation used in the same sentence typically causes coaches' heads to blow up). Coaching can be so powerful when a principal says something as simple as, "I have asked our coach, Steven, to meet

with each of you within the next two weeks to start a conver-sation around what kind of support you need in meeting our new district performance expectations. I will ask Steven to report back in two weeks with the names of the teachers that he has met with. Your work with Steven will be connected to my mid-year evaluation, so while he will not be made aware of your performance on your evaluation, you can use him as a tool to prepare for my observation."

2. Go to a really hot-shot teacher and tell her that you are learning to hone your high-flyer teacher coaching skill and you would love to work together to coach and be coached – simultaneously. You will be surprised at how rewarding supporting your teachers will be when *you* ask for help!

3. Encourage your principal to set up a minimum coaching ex-pectation. This would mean that, minimally, each teacher on the campus would have X number of coaching interactions each trimester or semester. Sometimes your leader has to force it.

4. Consider group coaching as a starting point. Perhaps you could pull a few hesitant, veteran teachers together and say, "I'd like to meet three times for 30 minutes each to talk about ways that you are incorporating the information from the last professional development session into your teaching." There can be safety in numbers to begin with, but note in later chap-ters how I outline group coaching as a short-term band-aid, not a long-term plan for success.

School Improvement and Capacity Building:
It Doesn't Have to Be So Difficult!

Originally appeared on www.jackson-consulting.com,
March 29, 2013

There is a lot of talk about fancy ways to build capacity and how to sustain school improvement efforts through capacity well-checks and measuring tools. While I think that these tools can be useful, what I'm really interested in is going beyond measuring capacity to BUILDING CAPACITY.

I don't want to oversimplify, but here's what it really boils down to: *We build capacity by habitually engaging in the activities that result in increased student achievement.*

Let me explain…

I have seen some very, um, how do I say this, *simplistic* school improvement efforts get fantastic results because the schools emphasized several things:

1. Staying the course by focusing on the heart of instruction and little else

2. Focusing on collaboration (both informally and more formally)

3. Continuing to use the data to identify: what is working and what isn't working?

The bottom line with our clients is that we want them to habitually (meaning many times throughout every school day) work their plans for school improvement. The habits that they build as they're improving their student performance and working their plans become second nature, really. And those successful habits are also addictive...they *feel* good because they get results. And when you *feel* good about something, you want to do them more often. (Psst...this is where the capacity is really built!)

So, when you're thinking about building capacity, avoid overly fussy and fancy tools and supposed tricks and ask your leadership team/ colleagues this question: *When we're working at full tilt, what does it look like?*

Make sure that your answers are built around *actions*. Examples could be: "We are using the weekly data to sort our kids for targeted interventions," or "We are using our planning time for collaboration on improving lessons." These actions become habits when you focus on them daily. And the habits lead to capacity.

And capacity leads to sustained improvement.

Step 1: Get Focused

If you have the guts to keep making mistakes,
your wisdom and intelligence leap forward with huge momentum.
~Holly Near

I have a love/hate relationship with the word "capacity." I love what it means, but I hate that we've so overused 'capacity' that it no longer holds any power. Somewhere in the handbook for all educators, there must be a chapter that starts, "When in doubt, throw in the word 'capacity' and people will think you know what you're talking about." I mean, if you were to ask one hundred educators what capacity meant, I think you'd get one hundred different answers – most of which let on to the fact that they had no clue what the word meant! The sad thing about throwing around the word capacity in an empty way is the fact that capacity is truly the key to sustained improvement across time. It's critical to the life of the school!

Here's my working definition of capacity-building: capacity-building is the work that a school does to build standard instructional habits from classroom to classroom, so much so that the habits become part of "how the school operates." And if the school is establishing the right habits that relate directly to improving the quality of the instruction, the whole school will be organized around the things that really matter most. They'll know capacity has been built when they engage enough in these habits that they see positive effects on student achievement in every classroom.

Capacity building is very tightly related to strong, sound and positive-outcome instructional habits. Capacity is also tightly related to having a few, very focused instructional targets. And coaching is a huge capacity building tool, especially when the coaching is pointed directly at the common practices that the entire school is working to build. If you've read my *Get a Backbone* book on leadership, you know that I advocate having no more than three instructional focus areas. Two would be even better.

So, how do we align our coaching practice to our capacity-building instructional focus areas? We ask ourselves a question that Richard Elmore taught me to ask: *Have I invoked the Principle of Reciprocity?*

Now you might be thinking, "Wait a minute! She's doing a switch-eroo on me! I thought she was going to talk to us in plain English, not fancy terms that need five dictionaries to decode!" Well, I am, but there is no better term to describe aligning coaching support to capacity-building than the "Principle of Reciprocity." The principle states: *anything that I ask you to do, I am required to give you the unit of capacity to be able to do it.* In other words, as a leader, if I am going to require you to pre-teach content to each of your below-benchmark kids next trimester, then I have to teach you to choose the right content to pre-teach to your below-benchmark kids. The school leader or principal sets up every teacher for successfully meeting his expectations.

Coaching is at the intersection of the leader's expectation and the teacher's capacity to carry out that expectation. We coach to build the capacity in teachers and skill level of teachers so they can carry out the principal's expectations. See how clean that is? Coaching isn't running around and coaching anything and everything, it's coaching teachers so that they can meet the expectations of their boss. It's really that simple.

Gut Check!

If your principal was reading that last paragraph over your shoulder along with you, what conversation would you need to have about his expectation and your coaching? Are you aligned? What is one action that your principal could take that would have massive impact on the quality of your coaching?

Here's an example of invoking the Principle of Reciprocity: We are implementing the Common Core State Standards and have, in response to the new Standards, adopted a new lesson planning form that every teacher will use to plan and upload into the system for review by the principal. Invoking the Principle of Reciprocity means that I take fully responsibility for teaching, modeling, practicing, applying and providing my teachers feedback via coaching on how to use the new lesson planning form. Once we go through many models and practice opportunities on the new form, I also am required to show you how to upload it into the system and give you tips and tricks as I watch you upload your first lesson plan.

When you invoke the Principle of Reciprocity, you are reinforcing that whatever you're teaching/modeling/practicing/applying/giving feedback on with your staff is an expectation. While we reinforce the instructional expectations, we also must remind our staff that coaching is for everyone and it's not optional. Even the most senior person on your staff will be working to build like-instructional habits that are designed to increase performance in every classroom. Coaching is a tool for getting the professional development into every classroom. In fact, I see the most accomplished teachers requesting coaching the most – they are excellent for a reason!

With that said, specific timing of coaching might vary, based upon need. It may be that some people are seen more often because they're struggling, and some people may be recruited to model for others because they've managed to become experts on a particular skill. Some people may need a lot more hand-holding than others. Others may not think they need hand-holding, but we have to go in there and provide it anyway.

When we fail to invoke the Principle of Reciprocity, school-wide initiatives fail. And they do not fail because there was not enough professional development, they fail because there was a lack of high-quality coaching and implementation *after* professional development. You see, the doing – the action – following professional development is the sole mark of quality training.

So, let's look a bit more closely as to exactly why professional development and coaching have failed to have wide-spread impact on the quality of teaching and the positive trajectory of student performance.

I have identified one main problem in many coaching programs: There is no formula for coaching.

In other words, nobody said "here's what coaching is, here's what's expected of you, here's what it needs to look like, and here's what it will look like when you're doing it well." Teachers often become resistant because they're thinking "I don't know what this coaching thing is!"

Coaching is too loose. When coaching does not have a form, teachers do not know what to expect in terms of time commitment, what goes in writing, what information stays between just the teacher and coach, and how often the coach will come around to give feedback. The interesting idea here is that oftentimes because coaches do not want to seem authoritative, they are free-flowing with the process... and it actually has the opposite effect! Teachers get frustrated because they don't know where they are in the process. This chapter was written to help you bring form to your coaching – and how to teach teachers what to expect from you as you coach.

But before I dive into the content, I want to tell you a little story.

I was working with a school district in the Northwest and they had spent a lot of money, a lot of time, and had done a lot of work on setting up their coaching program. What they decided to do with the middle school and high school coaching program was to assign part-time coaches that would coach their similar subject area peers. So, history/social studies teachers would coach other history/social studies teachers, for example.

In that district, we worked with five schools and four of the schools were working really hard to implement a very solid coaching model. The fifth school had little to no coaching happening during one of our mid-year visits. When we investigated further, here's what we found.

The coaches would tell me, "We really want to get people comfortable with the coaching role, so it doesn't feel like the teachers are being evaluated." They would do what I call "drive-bys" in the classrooms where they'd go into the classroom and go out. They didn't give any feedback and did not tell the teachers why they were in there. Nothing.

After some time, they found that the teachers were highly resistant. To combat this resistance, they decided to "stay out of the way." (By the way, I don't have any clue what that means!) They decided to do fewer drive-bys and go in and out less frequently, so as to not overwhelm the already skeptical teachers. The level of resistance increased. And during our mid-year visit, we were seeing more resistance and a decreased presence by the coaches in the classroom.

Here was the rub: the more the coaches stayed out of the classroom, the more resistance they saw and felt. And, the more resistance they saw, the more the coaches wanted to stay out of the classroom. This was highly frustrating. Finally, during one of my last visits with this particular school, I said, "Guys, I'm really frustrated. I don't understand why you're not getting into the classrooms. You're telling me the teachers are so resistant and I can't figure out why we can't get a handle on this after we've given you multiple steps to follow through on that would help you organize the coaching role."

Out of frustration, here's what I suggested to them: pull four of your most resistant teachers into a meeting tomorrow and allow me to interview them.

Well, the coaches practically fainted on the spot. The principal said she would do it, but she really didn't know whether it was a good idea. And one of the coaches even said, "Oh my gosh, please let me be absent tomorrow!"

You would have just laughed watching the whole scene the next day. We had four resistant teachers file into the library where our meeting was held. And the body language said it all! I'm not often intimidated, but even I was thinking, "Oh gosh, what have I done now?" And the coaches? They were huddled in the corner shivering.

I began by saying this to the four resistant and crabby teachers: "I have three very simple questions. The first question is what is coaching?" The teachers replied: "I don't know," "I'm not sure," "I'll tell you when I see it." The most resistant people had no clue what coaching was and what it was supposed to look like. We could fix that! The second question I asked them was, "How often are you coached?" All four of the biggest resistors answered similarly: "Never," "Mmm, I think somebody came through a couple of times," "I don't think I have a coach." So I turned to the coaches and I asked, "How often are you coaching these people?"

The coaches produced logs of how often they'd walked through those exact teacher's classrooms. And they had *technically* been in the classrooms. The thing was, they didn't do anything while they were in there – nor before or after for that matter! I told the coaches, "The disconnect here is you think you're coaching but you're leaving these people alone. What they're saying to you is, 'I'm really crabby about coaching because I don't know what it is and nobody's ever coached me and I don't trust what you guys are doing because I don't know what coaching is!'"

I stepped in at this point and explained what coaching is. "Coaching in your school is supporting teachers during instruction and ensuring that every teacher has similar ways of delivering the content across the school, across the departments and across the content areas." I explained that all of this was carried out with the goal of maximizing the output from the students.

And then I asked the teachers, "Do you think I'm wild and crazy to suggest that it probably behooves us to teach in similar ways, adjusted for our content?"

I also asked, "Do you agree with the fact that there are specific ways and techniques that we can use that will get great results in kids? Or even better results than some you might have gotten before? At the very least, do you agree with the fact that there are preferred methods of instruction?"

And every one of those four crabby, resistant, curmudgeons said, "Yes, I agree." Now, did they jump up and down and say, "Oh yes, we can't wait for coaching and we want it to start right now?" Not exactly, but they didn't say no. This was progress!

So, I turned to the coaches after the teachers left and said (with only a slight bit of frustration, of course!), "And what's the problem here?" They replied, "Well, you know, we wanted to tread lightly and you know we wanted to make sure we had buy-in and people felt 'heard.'"

I said, "Here's the deal. You have this group of people on your staff that is highly resistant. There are four. You have 64 on your staff. The other 60 are out there starving because you haven't given them structure – and you're focusing on these four. Get over it. You're going to win some, and lose some. Go for the win, that's number one. Second of all, you're surrounded by your crabbiest, most resistant people who have no idea what coaching is. Give them a structure for it and they're more likely to buy into it."

I continued, "Teaching adults is not like teaching kids. All you have to do with kids is get them excited about an idea and they're likely to come along with you. But adults are different. They want to know why and they want to know how. They want to know what it requires of them. They want to know the answer to the questions: "What is it going to look like? What does it look like when it works? What does it look like when it doesn't work? Why do we have to do this?"

My intervention for these coaches was to go back in and re-establish the form of coaching in that school – really help the staff understand what coaching was and wasn't and how it would look from here on out. You see, those coaches created resistance because they hung back. In trying to tread lightly, they caused their own demise. And I can say, even to this day they are struggling – it's hard to get back footing that was lost. It's not impossible, but it is difficult, especially when the coach struggles in the guts department!

Gut Check!

Identify and analyze the resistors on your campus. To what extent have you potentially contributed to their resistance? What action do you need to stop doing from this point on? What do you need to start doing?

My goal for you is that you are a coach who establishes a form for coaching and then follows that form so that your teachers know what to expect. And that's really all that we want to do for teachers right off the bat. From that point, our coaching job becomes to replicate that form again and again, and to let them know this is what it's going to look like when we're coaching together. It's really so simple to get folks on board with you – in fact, most are willing right now, but you've got to show them how it will all work.

You know, one of the most interesting things I've found about coaching is that in trying to "build buy-in," coaches will avoid giving feedback. They get into classrooms and write things in a notebook and take notes on what they're seeing, but they are intimidated about offering constructive criticism. And the very act of giving feedback late in the game is exactly what makes teachers feel like coaching is evaluative! When you're taking notes and visiting the classroom and never talking to or debriefing the teachers, they're likely assuming that you're running to the principal and saying, "Oh you're never going to believe what I saw in John's room!" You're not evaluating, but the lack of feedback sure makes it feel that way.

What this does highlight, however, is that coaches tend to struggle with how to get the ball rolling with coaching an individual teacher.

Even though I advocate a form for coaching, this does not mean that I believe that the coach needs to be in full control all the time – we would not build capacity through coaching if the coach did all of the work! I see that a hybrid model of the coach bringing structure to the coaching and the teacher being the central figure in carrying out the work is the only way to get results.

Here's what that might sound like: "Our principal has identified these three things as high priority focus areas for our school. Which one do you think you need the most support on, or with which one are you farthest along that we can refine?"

I believe in giving teachers options for coaching, but starting with, "So what would you like me to help you with?" is too vague. I suggest you go right in and say, "Here are the principal's goals, here are our school's goals and our district goals. Where is the most logical place to start?"

Now you may be thinking, "This is all well and good, but our principal doesn't have any goals!" Here's how we handle that: Make it up. Okay, not really. But you can say, "So you know that Principal Johnson has said several times that we're really focusing on improving the quality of our feedback to kids. How's that going? Where do you think we ought to start together?" This approach helps you to use even vague focus to create definition of the coaching role. I've seen this work well for coaches with a goal-less staff.

Perhaps you schedule a short time to chat with every teacher and ask them two priorities in the district and where they would like to start. Or you use the data as a conversation starter such as, "There are two trends in your grade level's data that show that we need to make adjustments…where would you like to start?"

Where I begin to get uneasy is when a coach asks a very open-ended question: "What would you like me to work on with you?" The answer to a broad question like that is typically that the teacher wants to work on something that they already know how to do! So by giving options, we see focus increase and resistance decrease. We have to get rid of the myth that if we give a form to coaching, or provide teachers with a focus, then we are being evaluative. That's just not true! In fact, if you are thinking, "I can't be direct with my teachers because they might think I'm evaluative," then you need to get over that right now. It's just not true.

So let's begin to build the structure of coaching right now.

First off, there are three phases of coaching:

1. The pre-conference

2. The action

3. The debriefing

These three phases make up the coaching cycle. Teachers will engage with you in multiple cycles of coaching throughout the school year.

We will work through each of these phases in a very detailed way, but here is a brief outline of each phase:

- **The pre-conference**. This is when you "broker the deal" for the coaching cycle. You establish what you will coach, how you will coach, when you will coach, what you will look for, when the debriefing will be, and what kind of notes you will take.

- **The action**. This is when you are in the classroom working with the teacher. There are five styles of coaching that will come into play during this phase: demonstration, observation, side-by-side, co-observation and shadow. You will choose which style (or styles) best fits the coaching outcome for that cycle.

- **The debriefing**. This is the real meat of the coaching cycle. This is when you review what you've seen and determine the action that will take place following the debrief. Without that set action, there is no reason to coach. Additonally, there will be no change in practice and the quality of instruction will not improve.

I want to be very clear from the beginning: If you are not debriefing a teacher, then you are not coaching. The bulk of the coaching happens during the debriefing. The debriefing is also the point at which the relationship between coach and teacher is built. So, you see why the resistant coaches in the story above were struggling to connect with their teachers – they weren't actually coaching!

Gut Check!

Are your debriefings moving teachers as much as you would like? Do your debriefings end with very specific action items for the teacher? If an outside observer were to come to your campus and ask each of your teachers what they were focusing on with you, would they know?

Next, we need to look at how to begin the coaching cycle.

There are six methods to jump-start coaching:

1. The one-legged interview

2. The open ended concerns statement

3. Using data

4. Following up on professional development

5. Sharing work that you've done with other teachers

6. Following up on a team meeting

I know, "one-legged interview" sound very odd! The reason why it is called a one-legged interview is because you're gathering information while walking one leg at a time. The one-legged interview is informal. Here's an example: When coming out of the teacher's lounge, I notice that Heather is walking next to me and I say, "Hey Heather, how is that new writing curriculum going for you? How are you feeling about it?"

We're walking (one leg at a time) and I just listen. She might say, "Oh it's going really well but gosh it's taking so much time to prep and it's hard for me to get everything together and..." I'm just listening, at this point, but then I go back to my notes in my office and I jot down "3-23-13 – Heather seems to be overwhelmed with the amount of prep for the writing program."

So the next time I'm trying to go in and figure out where I'm going to start with her, I'll say, "You know Heather I was thinking about the other day when we were walking back from lunch and I asked you about how the new writing program was going. You said you know it's going pretty well but the prep is really heavy. Let's talk about that. How can I support you in managing the prep?"

And, boom! You're into phase one. That's what a one-legged interview is all about: a casual conversation. On a side note, it's amazing how many coaches I've worked with that are never in the staff room – the very place that teachers are venting, discussing, debriefing and sharing ideas. That's a great place for you to listen. Just listen. Don't worry about coaching, just worry about listening.

The second way that we gather information to begin our coaching is through something called an "open-ended concerns statement." (NOTE: my love for sticky notes and note cards will begin to emerge here!) To design an open-ended concerns statement, consider what it is that you're implementing and design two open-ended questions around that. Then, talk with your principal about using two minutes of your next staff meeting to gather some information from the staff regarding those open-ended questions. Notice that I said two minutes. You want to get your staff's initial gut check reactions to these questions, so make it brief.

Here's what that might sound like at a staff meeting: "So in front of you, you have an index card. On the front side of the index card I'd like for you to jot down your biggest struggle with implementing our new Common Core Standards. (NOTE: these questions are related to your instructional focus areas at the school, since that is our primary coaching focus). You have thirty seconds to do this. Now, on the flipside I want you to write how I can help you with that."

Sometimes I'll ask them to jot down their quick responses to questions like these: What's your biggest road block from figuring this out? If you could fix one thing about this Common Core Standards implementation what would it be?

I find that when I give the teachers too long to respond or if I hand out the cards to be completed prior to the meeting, the answers are almost too thought out. I start to get the politically correct responses! I want the real, raw answers to my questions so that I can continue to focus my coaching support to the teachers. If they're not giving me their real responses, then my coaching could be off-target. Off-target coaching is another breeding ground for resistance.

Then, I collect the cards and I start to sort them according to what the teachers are feeling, what they're struggling with, what they feel like they're doing well, or what their road blocks might be. What I begin to see are patterns of needs.

When I analyze the index card responses, I might find that an over-whelming number of teachers have listed "time" as the thing that gets in the way of them carrying out the professional development. Another time when I ask them to respond, I might find that teachers are falling into two categories as we implement a new curriculum: some feel like it's way too difficult for our English Language Learners, while others are feeling like they are having to give up too much of their "old" content to teach the new program.

Since the teachers have given me insight on how I can help them, all I have to do is follow up! And the coaching process has begun.

My next conversation is with an individual teacher, and it might sound something like, "Hey, you know, I was looking at all the data that I picked up when we filled out those index cards. I realized that a lot of teachers are struggling with managing their time during the implementation of our new reading program. I'd like to help you with that. What's your biggest struggle?"

And I'm in!

Some other coaching starter conversations are:

- Using data to jump-start a coaching conversation: "You know, as I was reviewing our school data, I noticed that your department was struggling to help the kids master the vocabulary portion of the weekly assessment. Talk to me about that. Did you notice that? Why do you think that is? Where can we start to work on that?"

- Following up on professional development to jump-start a coaching conversation: "Tell me, what are the things you said you picked up from our math training on Thursday? How can I support you in getting started on that?"

- Sharing work that you've done with other teachers to jump-start a coaching conversation: "I was working with the seventh grade English teachers on getting students to respond in writing to an open-ended prompt – would that be something we could work on in your English class?"

- Following up on a team meeting to jump-start individual coaching: "Hey, I wanted to follow up with you on our last team meeting. How is your pre-teaching of the vocabulary to the English Language Learners going? Are you seeing improvement in their comprehension of the text?"

So, to review, there are six methods to jump-start coaching:

- The one-legged interview

- The open ended concerns statement

- Using data

- Following up on professional development

- Sharing work that you've done with other teachers

- Following up on a team meeting

Here's the great news: you only have to start the coaching process once! After your first coaching cycle with a teacher, your debriefing, will roll right into your next coaching cycle. More to follow on that.

Connect Your Coaching to the Common Core

Make an appointment right now with your principal. Take one hour to map out which domains of the Common Core you will be coaching this school year. For example, in August, September and October, focus on coaching the RI Standards. November through February, focus on coaching the SL Standards.

By prioritizing the Common Core content with your leader, you will link your coaching to the number one instructional challenge on your teachers' plates: The Common Core. Your coaching will help them stay the course and avoid getting scattered and overwhelmed.

Coaching Through Those Sticky Situations

Facebook fan Toni W. asks: *How do I handle staff members that need to make change, but refuse to, and an administrator that leaves it up to me to make the change happen?*

Well Toni, first I think you ought to sneak a copy of *Get a Backbone, Principal* into your leader's stack of summer reading this year! All promotion aside, it sounds like you are describing a leader that is either too weak to set an expectation of coaching for the entire staff, or totally misunderstands the powerful effect coaching can have.

Either way, here are a few words of wisdom I can give you:

Go directly to the principal and say, "I need your help with something. I need you to remind the staff at the next meeting that coaching with me is not optional. This will make my coaching go so much smoother and will allow me to have an even greater impact on the quality of the teaching here."

Act as if you have been given ultimate coaching power (this is my personal favorite!) by saying, "As you know, Mrs. Hannah, our principal, has set 'increasing the engagement of all students' as an instructional focus this year. I am going to come to talk with each of you individually about a good starting point in meeting Mrs. Hannah's goals for us." This works surprisingly well!

You have to divide and conquer if you don't have a leader with a backbone. What that means is that you must determine the teachers with whom you can have the biggest impact with the least amount of leadership backbone needed…and start there. Without the principals' blessing, you just won't win certain teachers over to coaching. And, quite honestly, I don't want you to waste your valuable coaching time on folks who have no intention of being coached. Go for the win – and start with folks who are almost ready for coaching or totally ready for it.

Set up a regular time each week to meet with your principal. This should be a 20-minute meeting that is focused simply on taking your staff roster and spending one minute discussing the instructional focus/coaching focus for that teacher. I find that regularly meeting boosts the connection between leadership and coaching work – and a lack of regular principal/coach collaboration does the opposite.

STOP "GOING TO" PROFESSIONAL DEVELOPMENT AND START "DOING IT!"

Originally appeared on www.jackson-consulting.com, March 11, 2013

So I just got off the phone with a potential client who said this to me in the middle of the call, "What I'd really like you to do is lead a discussion on a chapter of a book that we're reading. And then if you could tie it back to the Title I workshop that we attended a few weeks back, that'd be great."

I have to say, I was a bit perplexed by this because the reason this person called me in the first place was because they were in Year 3 of school improvement, and it just didn't seem like the most important thing to do was to read a chapter and discuss it. Or even to tie the discussion to a workshop.

Here's why:

First off, lots of our clients are in school improvement or heading there – that's why they call us. So that fact wasn't as striking. The most striking part of that request was that they were going to *talk* about doing stuff, but they weren't interested in *doing* stuff.

Now, I happen to know that this person who contacted me is a very good administrator with lots of great feedback from other colleagues (that's how we got in touch with each other). I know that he is very motivated and interested in doing the right thing – and, most importantly – is interested in doing right by the kids. The staff and the principal just haven't quite figured out what aspect of the work they should be doing that will have the biggest impact on kids.

Essentially, they are stuck in the "we've got to get some more professional development before we can do it" mode. It's almost like schools in this position need a "blessing" from a trainer, presenter or author to do exactly what they already know they need to do. I felt like during the conversation, though, he knew exactly what his school needed to be doing. I can kind of relate to needing an "expert" to confirm what I already know.

Let me explain…

A while ago, we decided to create a new website – one that would be way more interactive, user friendly and one that could be updated multiple times a day without a web designer. So, we went looking for "the best" in the field.

And we found her.

Supposedly.

We started the long, arduous (but also fun!) process of getting our website together – content, graphics, themes, colors, etc. About two weeks in, things started to seem kind of off – the communication was breaking down, some of our tried-and-true ideas were getting shot down, even though our gut told us it was the right thing to do. Ultimately, we had to bid farewell to this web designer and pinch hit with another to finish the job. It wasn't going to work.

It was a mess, but here was the deal: Just because we weren't web design experts, didn't mean we didn't know what we needed and what was going to be right for our readers and clients. In fact, we *did* know, we just needed input and ideas from the experts to *complement* what we already knew to be true and necessary. We needed help (along with solid input) putting our plan into action.

The big idea is this: books, trainers and experts are useful *if you know yourself and what you need.*

And you don't have to wait for experts or authors to "bless" your school improvement ideas before you get started. Sometimes the experts are there to birth an idea for you or get you unstuck along the way to your final goal. Most of us can get stuck in the realm of getting started. And sometimes we need a push into action.

So as I meandered through the call with the potential client I basically said this, "Do you really want me to come and lead a book study that you could lead on your own? Or do you need help translating all of your professional development and all of your readings into action?"

Well, let's just say, I'm on a plane in a few months to help them get started and put it into action.

Step 2: Get into the Flow

By 'guts' I mean grace under pressure.
~Ernest Hemingway

A couple of years ago I fulfilled a life-long dream to vacation in Tokyo. One of the things that I was interested in experiencing was the order of it all. I love an organized space – in fact I'm the type that wants you to look in my cupboard and drawers because I'm proud of how organized they are (I know, gag!)! When I hopped off the plane in Tokyo, I was immediately struck by how there is a general flow of getting things done: from meeting people arriving on different flights, to going through customs, from meeting my driver in a certain spot, to walking across the street and getting out of the parking structure. It all had a flow. And, most impressively, everyone followed that flow!

What that flow, as I'm calling it, enabled me to do was to focus on the beauty of the city. I didn't have to worry about where I was going to queue up for the train because everyone queued up in the same place – I just had to follow the crowd, allowing me to focus on where my next stop was. When I was doing some shopping in the Harajuku district, I didn't have to worry about when to cross the street or which side of the street to walk down, because everyone did the same thing – all I had to do was focus on the next pair of shoes I was buying! Order brought comfort as I traveled in a place where I literally had not one clue about the language.

The same is true about coaching: order brings comfort. And an agreed-upon flow of coaching allows us to spend our time working on, grappling with, fussing over and discussing the content of the coaching. And as we learned in Chapter 1, the content of the coaching is improving the quality of instruction.

We've clearly established at this point that coaching, in order to be effective and measureable, has to follow a form. In Chapter 2, I outlined for you the three phases of coaching:

- **The pre-conference:** This is where you "broker the deal" for the coaching cycle. You establish what you will coach, how you will coach, when you will coach, what you will look for, when the debriefing will be and what kind of notes you will take.

- **The action:** This is where you are in the classroom working with the teacher. There are five styles of coaching that will come into play during this phase of coaching: demonstration, observation, side-by-side, co-observation and shadow. You will choose which style best fits the coaching outcome for that cycle.

- **The debriefing:** This is the real meat of the coaching cycle. This is where you debrief and determine the action that will take place following the debriefing.

Let's start by unpacking each of the phases.

The Pre-Conference

The pre-conference is all about the set-up. It's like the logistical meeting-of-the-minds prior to an interaction. The pre-conference is where you follow up on information and use one of the six conversation starters from Chapter 2:

1. The one-legged interview

2. The open ended concerns statement

3. Using data

4. Following up on professional development

5. Sharing work that you've done with other teachers

6. Following up on a team meeting

You'll use the conversation starters to get a commitment to coaching. You want to ask questions that nail down the following:

- When will I come in?

- What will be the focus of the coaching?

- What style of coaching will we engage in?

- Where will the coaching take place?

- What kind of notes will we take?

- How long will this coaching interaction take?

- When will the debriefing take place?

- Where will the debriefing take place?

The goal of the pre-conference is to set every single logistical piece in the right place so that you can – finish my sentence here – that's right, focus on the quality of the teaching.

So, here's what the end result of a strong pre-conference might sound like:

"Okay, so on Tuesday at 10:15, I'll come into your classroom and we will look at your vocabulary work from 10:15 to 10:30. I'll sit at the side of the classroom that lets me be closest to your ELL kids. I'll focus really specifically on capturing notes on their responses to your teaching of the new vocabulary words – especially when they're using those new words in a discussion about the text you're reading. Then, we'll come together at 3:45 p.m. tomorrow to debrief what I found and look at ways that we might be able to get even more power out of those vocabulary lessons. Deal?"

Let's look at what that conversation helps the teacher to understand (and helps limit resistance):

- What the coach will be looking for

- Where the coach will be sitting

- Who the coach will be watching

- What the coach will be writing down

- How much time is required of the teacher

- What the expectation is around this coaching interaction

- When the teacher can expect feedback on the teaching

The one commitment that I want you to make right now is to scheduling the debriefing during the pre-conference. I find that once I head back to my office, things get in the way: I have five calls to return, I get stuck on an email, I get hooked on a technology issue, I head over to a different grade level to help them print the scores only to find that the printer's broken. And meanwhile I've gone into the class, worked with the teacher, taken a bunch of notes and they never get feedback on the teaching.

I certainly don't mean to skip the debriefing, but things naturally get in the way.

I don't know about you, but when somebody would come into my classroom, and I didn't know what they were looking for and what they were jotting down, I automatically assumed that they were crafting my firing notice. I thought I was a goner!

So, you see how putting structure to the coaching eases fears in teachers – there is no "gotcha!" from the coaching process. It's all laid out long before it even begins.

I am willing to go out on a limb right now and say that if you implemented just what you've learned about how to set the stage of coaching, how to get started with a focus, and how to structure the first phase of coaching, nearly all of the resistance to coaching that you might be experiencing would nearly or entirely go away. My big revelation from all these years of coaching others is this: *if I give teachers the coaching structure, we have more time to focus on the content of the coaching. And when we have more time on the content of the coaching, the quality of the instruction improves.*

One hot coaching topic is how to handle teachers that ask to see my notes. As a practice, I don't give my notes to everyone because I feel that if I offer my notes, then that actually appears evaluative, because it's so similar to a teacher evaluation by a principal. However, if seeing my notes is going to help a teacher understand that I am taking notes simply on what I'm seeing, not what I'm thinking, then I will gladly put a copy of the notes in their box. I would never want my note-taking to become a bone of contention between a teacher and myself. By showing the notes, I can let the teacher know that I'm not judging their teaching and turning the notes into the principal – I'm merely capturing the facts on the teaching and learning during their lesson. More to follow in Step 4 about what to document during an observation.

On the flip side, I've encountered a few situations where, in order to avoid the entire note-taking conversation, there has been a "no note-taking by the coach" directive. I'm going to be really frank with you. If you're not taking notes in the classroom because you feel like it's going to offend a teacher, or it seems too evaluative, you're on the wrong track. If taking notes is a real problem then, trust me, you've got bigger issues that extend beyond note-taking.

If you're experiencing resistance to note-taking, I encourage you to return to Chapter 1 and talk with your leadership team about setting the expectations of coaching. If the goal of note-taking is to capture what is going on in the classroom from an objective standpoint, then trying to remember what you've seen because you can't take notes is going to accomplish just the opposite: it will feel evaluative because it appears to come directly from the coach's thoughts, not the coach's notes.

So now we're on to our second step in the coaching cycle: the action.

Basically "the action" is the carrying out of what you said you were going to do in segment number one, minus the debriefing. As mentioned previously, there are five styles of coaching:

1. Demonstration

2. Observation

3. Side-by-side

4. Co-observation

5. Shadow coaching

Here is a detailed look at the five styles of coaching that will take place during the second phase of the coaching process:

Style 1: Demonstration

The most underused, yet one of the most results-driven, forms of coaching is the coach demonstration. This style of coaching strikes fear in the hearts of many, many coaches because they think, "Who am I to go in and demonstrate a lesson?" Think about this: if we know that in order for anyone to learn something new, they have to be taught, modeled, guided, given feedback and then moved to application, then we have to practice that during our coaching of new techniques in the classroom. Modeling is a really big part of that explicit teaching of the teacher.

If you are insecure modeling lessons (and I'm not advocating that you model on the fly, but that your modeling has some lead time with at least a day of prep time) then that will inhibit your coaching power. Period.

When a coach shows a teacher how to do something *with their own kids*, the teacher tends to have a higher implementation rate of the skill that was modeled. Your value as a coach is predicated on your ability and willingness to demonstrate in the classrooms – it's where your credibility and relationships with teachers are built.

Word to the wise: It is very common that as I am coaching teachers, they will request to see me demonstrate the entire class period – anywhere between 40-90 minutes. Now, while I know that seems like that would be incredibly helpful, what I also know is that after about 20-25 minutes, people start to check out. I often say they start jotting down the things they need to do after school, they start thinking up new recipes, or doing crossword puzzles and Sudoku!

What you want to do is demonstrate a small chunk of instruction (typically about 30 minutes) so that they can pick up a couple of ideas that they can take right back to their own classroom.

As the demonstrator, I will take care of all management, all behavior and all teaching, so that the observer can literally script what they're seeing without feeling like they need to jump in and help co-manage the class with me. What I want to demonstrate is the connection between the management, the engagement, and the instruction and how that all comes together. That's the magic of a demonstration – we are showing our teachers how the planning, preparation, delivery, feedback, engagement, enthusiasm and skills of teaching all work simultaneously. If traditional forms of professional development, like the "sit and get," had high rates of implementation, then there would be no need for demonstration. But we know that traditional professional development isn't enough – the coaching must happen in the classroom, not the training room.

Style 2: Observation

This is the most common form of coaching. The coach enters the classroom to observe the teacher and students on a portion of the lesson and take notes on what is seen. Later, the coach debriefs what he saw with the teacher. Observation is the most traditional form of coaching and definitely not impactful enough on its own.

There are two types of observation: formal and informal. When we're talking about the full coaching cycle, we are referring to the more formal observation that will result in debriefing and action steps. An informal observation is when I am popping in and out of classrooms without a pre-conference. What I'm looking for during these short bursts of observation are themes of instruction across several classrooms. I might visit six classrooms in an hour to check and see how their engagement levels are. I might go into one grade level's classrooms for 5-7 minutes each, as I check to see how their introduction to the new chapter is going. I am not obligated to give feedback during these informal observations, but they will likely lead to more formal coaching cycles, as I will take the information that I gather during these informal pop-ins and follow up with teachers during the pre-conference.

Style 3: Side-by-side

During side-by-side coaching, the coach and the teacher jointly prepare for the lesson. The teacher remains in control of the class, while the coach is sitting very close to the teacher during the teaching. As the teacher is instructing the kids, the coach is sitting and literally giving whispered feedback such as, "Try that again, you didn't have everybody there," or "Go back and just check and see what these kids are saying back here," or "Let's go ahead and model that one more time, I'm not sure they're solid enough on that yet."

Side-by-side coaching is exactly what a coach does on the sidelines during a sports game: feedback in the moment. Teachers do not have to wait for a full-blown debriefing because we've corrected some of the work right there in the classroom and they have an opportunity to "fix it up" in real time. The number one question that teachers have around side-by-side coaching is "won't my kids think it's weird?" And my answer to that is the kids won't think it's weird if you tell them it's not weird.

In fact, during the pre-conference I role-play with teachers the kind of conversation that they can have with their kids, and it goes like this: "Ladies and gentlemen, we are going to try something a bit different today. At 10:15 our math coach, Mrs. B is going to come into our classroom and do some work with me while you are learning how to do fractions. At first it might seem a little weird that she and I will be talking to each other during the lesson, but you'll soon get used to it. What I want you to do is 'business as usual.' I'll still be your teacher and you'll still do the work that I ask you to do. The only difference is that Mrs. B and I will have some side conversations. If we're having a side conversation, I want you to just sit quietly until I start teaching again. There might be a moment when Mrs. B takes over the teaching – this is my way of learning some new things about teaching. Make sense? Good!"

It's really that simple.

I made a rookie coaching mistake once and I want you to learn from it. I was modeling how to use different coaching techniques with a group of coaches. The host coach had done the pre-conferences with the teachers so that I could jump right in and do the action and debriefing while the coaches watched. During one of my model classrooms, I understood that the coach had established with the teacher that we were going to do side-by-side approach. So as the teacher was teaching, I made a little motion with my hand like, "Is it alright if I jump in here?" Well, there was a miscommunication and the teacher did not know that I was going to side-by-side coach. And well, let's just say that didn't go so well. The teacher had every right to be upset with me for barging in on the lesson – I wouldn't want anyone doing that to me! So, I apologized and then went to the debriefing room with the group of observing coaches and said, "See why you must pre-establish your style of coaching?"

While it was an honest mistake, it was a pretty serious one. When I went to go and talk with the teacher at the end of the day, she was still quite upset with me and I didn't blame her one bit. This style of coaching is so powerful, but it can also be very personal. We need to handle it carefully so that we aren't stepping on toes and jeopardizing the coaching relationships that we've worked so hard to build.

Gut Check!

How often are you using side-by-side coaching? If it is not part of your regular coaching routine, then commit to adding it in right away! List three teachers right now that would be great candidates for side-by-side coaching with you.

Style 4: Co-observation

Co-observation is the coaching style where I take the teacher that I'm coaching into a different classroom to observe the host teacher using the same technique that the observing teacher is learning about.

During my pre-conference I might have a conversation that goes something like this: "Hey, I know we're working on boosting discussion. I would like to suggest that we go see Ryan in class seven, because he's doing an excellent job during his lab with boosting discussion. How about I set that up with Ryan and we can go in for a 30-minute demonstration of that on Monday. I can get you coverage during that time, or we can try to get into his classroom during your prep period. What do you think?"

I have not had a teacher turn down the opportunity to go and observe another teacher for a specific purpose. In fact, they're usually very enthusiastic about it. Notice, however, I didn't say, "I'll cover your class while you go in and observe Ryan." During co-observation, I am sitting right next to the observing teacher, and we are actually having conversations about the teaching while it's happening. It's actually quite like side-by-side coaching while we're co-observing.

Once you establish that co-observation is your next step, you must have this kind of conversation with the host teacher: "Ryan, I'm bringing Thomas in to watch you do the lesson on boosting discussion that I observed the other day. So I want to make sure when we come in you're doing that same thing. When are you doing that next?" You want to make sure that what you are bringing the observing teacher to actually observe is what she will see!

Now, this last step of the co-observation style is one of capacity building. Here's what it sounds like:

"Hey Ryan, I'd love for you to walk Thomas through how you developed the practice of boosting discussion in your classroom. Would you join us at our debriefing of your lesson on Thursday at 1:30?" I've now linked two teachers together, led them into a focused conversation about their teaching. What is very likely to happen in the future, is that the observing teacher bypasses me altogether and goes directly to the modeling teacher and asks questions. Now that's Capacity Building 101!

I have had tremendous success with co-observation for several reasons:

1. I'm building the capacity of the team by highlighting the support that teachers can provide each other

2. I'm using other teachers as models, which is a huge confidence booster for the staff

3. I'm not setting myself up as the only one who can give feedback and coaching to teachers

4. I'm providing a real-time look at teaching by those who do it every day

5. I'm building unofficial mentors or models within a building

I believe that everybody on campus is good at something. And it's about time that we go beyond our own tried-and-true superstar teachers and start to find opportunities for mentoring and modeling outside of the usual suspects. I'll bet you will be quite excited by what you find when you try this capacity-building form of coaching.

Style 5: Shadow Coaching

Shadow coaching is the most intense form of coaching, reserved for your most struggling teachers. I use shadow coaching only when I've tried all other types of coaching, and the teacher is having trouble translating what they've seen demonstrated and turning it into practice in their classroom.

I begin by co-planning a very small (15 minutes) portion of the lesson with the teacher. When I get into the classroom, I teach the first one or two minutes, they teach the exact same one or two or three minutes – they literally mimic me. What we're trying to force through shadow coaching is that the teacher feels what a particular technique is like during instruction. This is especially important for teachers who are having difficulty applying what they're seeing. You might be thinking, "Oh that will never work with my kids!" They are applying something new in a very controlled environment with me right by their side, literally prepping the class with my instruction before they demonstrate their own.

However, please understand that you must do this in extremely small chunks. If a teacher is needy enough to require shadow coaching, then we know that we have to provide them with small wins. That's what shadow coaching is about: very small pieces of instruction that we weave together across time.

So here's where we stand: we have outlined the pre-conference and the five styles of coaching. That leads us to the debriefing. The debriefing is where the real coaching takes place, and it is so important that we have dedicated a whole chapter to providing feedback. But before we move to that chapter, I want to set the stage for the debriefing, or prompting reflection.

There are two parts of the debriefing:

1. **Reflection on the teaching**: This is the commitment to increasing the quality of the instruction.

2. **Reflection on the coaching process**: This is the commitment to continually improving the relationship between teacher and coach.

> ### Gut Check!
>
> We know that a strong coaching program matches the style of coaching to the need of the teacher. If I were to look at your coaching calendar, would it represent the fact that you are tailoring support to teachers? Or are you a one-size-fits-all kind of coach?

In our next chapter, we will get very specific about structuring feedback and giving feedback in a way that it will lead to action back in the classroom (this is "reflection on the teaching"). But the often forgotten reflection is one that begins with these questions: "How do you think our coaching is going?" or "Is there a way for us to work more efficiently and effectively together?" or "How can I better serve you in my coaching role?" When we reflect on the coach/teacher relationship, we are able to clear the debris from past coaching interaction and possible mistakes. While you might not ask this question every time you end a debriefing, you certainly want to check-in with a teacher every month or so to see what work can continue to be done on the relationship level.

I cannot emphasize enough the idea that folks will work with you when they feel like you are worthy of working with. If they trust you, they will allow you to coach them – even if they really don't want to!

There are five parts to building trust in the coaching role:

1. You must be visible and keep your appointments

2. You must be trustworthy and keep conversations confidential

3. You must allow them to make mistakes and recover from them

4. You must be able to model and practice what you preach

5. You must regularly give feedback through a structured coaching practice

One of the questions I am asked so often about coaching is, "How do I get my teachers to trust me?" The answer is you don't. Trust comes from knowing someone deeply and learning that they are deserving of your trust. Expecting that teachers will trust you before you've had the chance to earn their trust is simply a waste of time. Just get started on the coaching – and they will trust you because you prove that you are trustworthy.

Show them that you allow them to make mistakes and that you can laugh and move forward. Show them that, while you may have private conversations with the principal, that you aren't sharing private coaching information. Show them that when you say you'll be in to observe or debrief, you value their time by actually doing what you've committed to. Show them that you follow a plan of coaching and, because you have a plan, are able to totally delete the "gotcha" mentality of past coaching programs. The operative word is "show." The trust is in the *doing* of coaching.

Connect Your Coaching to the Common Core

Analyze with teacher teams what past practices will need to stay in place as you implement the Common Core Standards. Ask them to think about which practices will need to be let go, in light of the Common Core. During your team and department meetings, systematically bring new Common Core-related practices to the team and teach, model, practice and apply them with the team *before* they are responsible for rolling the practices into the classroom. This is an opportunity to practice what we preach!

Coaching Through Those Sticky Situations

Facebook fan, Stacie S. asks: *How do I balance the teachers wanting to take baby steps toward improvement with the fact that their students don't have time to wait?*

Stacie, this is the age-old coaching frustration! Where I think we can best support teachers in moving faster instructionally, is by helping them figure out the baby steps that are going to get them there. Let me explain: If we know that teachers need to pre-teach a certain strategy to their struggling kids, but they feel like they should wait until second semester to do that because the kids are learning so much new content and they don't want to overwhelm them, then we need to break it into small chunks.

I, like you, would have liked the pre-teaching to start the second day of school, but that's just not what is happening for this team. So, I start by brainstorming everything that needs to be done to pre-teach the lesson to the neediest kids. Here's my list:

- Determine who needs to be pre-taught

- Determine what parts of my lessons need to be pre-taught (and hold the most critical skills)

- Determine how I will pull the small group aside for pre-teaching

- Determine what the kids not pulled to the small group will be doing during the small group time

- Determine the behavioral expectations and steps to getting kids working independently

- Determine how often I will switch the group that I pre-teach and how I will figure out who needs to be added and deleted from the group

Then I would tackle 1-2 of the bulleted items each week until I have full implementation of the small groups, in this case.

What I see so often is that teachers struggle to break down how to go from their current practice to what you are suggesting – they get stuck with the "how do I do this?" question. Your coaching can help them not only get from point A to point B without losing their minds, but it can also help them learn how to attack a challenge and get 'er done.

GETTING AWAY FROM THE "GOTCHA!" OF TEACHER EVALUATION

Originally appeared on www.jackson-consulting.com, January 28, 2013

I had a meeting last week with my mentor and our conversation throughout the day rolled around the idea of teacher evaluation. She taught me that "teacher evaluation" is going to take on a whole new meaning...and it's about time.

Here are some thoughts we batted around:

- Teacher evaluation has to turn from a "gotcha!" (as in "gotcha doing something wrong") into a very important step in tailoring professional development for teachers

- Teacher evaluation is going to be one of the first steps in designing "individualized teacher plans" for professional development

- Long gone should be the "one-size-fits-all" type of professional development – we MUST take into account our staff's individual experience, expertise and skill

- Individualized professional development plans are going to require principals and coaches to have a much higher knowledge of how to diagnose and prescribe teacher professional development programs

- Our greatest asset is our teaching staff. We have to cultivate, weed and prune our talent pool, just as any other field does

So let me play these thoughts out for a minute here.

I am a 7th grade teacher who has some struggles with lesson planning. My general teaching skill is pretty darn good, but in terms of creating cohesive lessons and mini-assessments for my content, I don't have that skill. During an observation, my principal and coach realize that my delivery is solid, but when I have to create lessons where curriculum guides don't exist, the overall complexity of my lessons is at about the 4th grade level.

In the "old" way of teacher evaluation, I would receive feedback (typically in written form) from my principal, detailing the problems in my lesson.

And that's it.

Yep, try figuring out what happens next! Try getting some real coaching! In fact, I'm not quite sure what kind of support I even need! Help!

Under the "new and improved" paradigm of teacher evaluation, my principal and coach would meet with me and talk through the lesson, asking me lots of questions about my preparation practices, from where I pull my materials, and where I believe my lesson struggles originate. We would probably identify together that I need some lesson planning support and would be invited to the coach's weekly "lesson plan retreat" that's held after school for teachers who need some hand-holding in this area. My other department colleagues wouldn't necessarily attend this training/coaching session because their needs are different than mine.

In fact, I teach next to Mr. Tate. He's an excellent teacher, but this year he has a bunch of Gifted and Talented kids in his classroom for the first time. When he met with the principal to make his quarterly goals, his number one goal was to learn about techniques for his science class that are particularly supportive of the Gifted and Talented kids. So, the coach approaches Mr. Tate and lets him know that the district is running a three-week webinar about how to plan lessons specific to Gifted and Talented kids. He signs up, and even comes and shares information with me after every class!

This is true differentiated evaluation as professional development.

Nowhere in that scenario do you hear, "You WHAT? You don't KNOW that?!?" The response from the leadership is, "I'll get you help so that you can move along in your mastery of teaching skills."

I'm sure you're thinking, "Oh my gosh, this is going to take so much coordination." Yep, it is. But it's going to become *how* we think when we act with a tailoring mindset.

I think we've clung to traditional "everyone gets the same thing" professional development because it FELT like we were really doing something special – like we were actually giving people what they needed to become more efficient and effective in the classroom.

But the truth is, no matter how you slice it, our classroom teachers have all kinds of different needs!

We can't possibly say that 90-plus percent of professional development needs are the same for every teacher, can we?

So, here's my encouragement to you as you prepare for what, no doubt, will be the future of teacher evaluation: Chart out all of the different resources you have *right now* that would help you differentiate professional development.

Second step? Create a very simple survey for your teachers that give them an opportunity to respond freely to these questions:

- What is the number one thing getting in the way of your teaching of the content?

- What kind of professional development do you think would be helpful in combating that "in the way" thing?

- What type of professional development leaves you feeling like you really learned a lot on a new/semi-new topic?

Just the answer to these simple questions will help you begin to tailor your school's PD. And that's a great start!

Step 3: Get to the Dance of the Debrief

Anybody with a little guts and the desire to apply himself can make it.
He can make anything he wants to make of himself.
~Willie Shoemaker

This chapter is one that is critical for your success as a coach – and it contains information that will help debunk the "It's scary to give feedback!" myth. Let's be very clear: If you are not giving focused, direct feedback to teachers about their teaching, then you are not coaching. I evaluate the effectiveness of a coach's work by the breadth and depth of the feedback he gives to the teachers. After all, it's that very feedback and coaching that takes professional development right into the classroom. And the classroom is where we see the effect of professional development on student achievement.

I have seen many coaching models where the focus is on the teacher doing the reflection and choosing the content. Of course, it's critical to involve the teachers in the coaching process. After all, that's where the relationship is built. But when we leave the content and the focus of coaching directly up to the teacher, we are missing out on the very power of coaching: perspective.

Let's be frank: there is more resistance to a lack of feedback and debriefing of teaching than there is to receiving feedback. So many coaches I work with fear that, if they give specific feedback to a teacher on what to alter, the teacher will feel evaluated. What I see is actually the opposite. When a coach fails to give feedback, the teacher fantasizes that the coach is going to the principal and spilling all of her guts about the horrid teaching that she saw in the room, and that, jointly, they're writing up the resignation letter that they'll force the teacher to sign later!

Before we debrief and give feedback on the teaching, we have to establish very directly with teachers this idea: Formal evaluation is when someone comes into your room, uses an official form, takes notes, and turns in those notes to someone in a leadership position who has the power to hire and fire. And, as your coach, I'm not going to do that. I might take notes, but they will be informal. I might talk with our principal about whether I'm coaching you or not, but our coaching together will be tied into the principal's instructional goals for the school, so what I'm coaching you on is not a mystery at all. I will provide you specific recommendations about how to improve the effects of your teaching, but it is ultimately your choice as to whether you incorporate them into your teaching.

Even with a great coaching set-up, though, providing feedback takes guts. It takes guts to give someone corrective feedback. Just the term "corrective feedback" can make coaches nervous.

Gut Check!

Is there one teacher on your staff that makes you nervous to debrief? Keep that teacher in mind as you read this chapter. That person is your motivation for mastering the art of the debrief.

But I'm going to let you in on a little secret: providing feedback does not have to be scary. You are going to show your teachers a formula that you'll use as you debrief them, so there will be no mystery and no "switcheroo" or hidden agenda. There is order to a debrief or feedback session that the teachers will grow to expect, and that will take some of the nervousness away for both the coach and teacher.

Here is the flow of the debriefing:

1. Restate the purpose for the coaching interaction

2. Ask the teacher to reflect on the teaching

3. Using your notes, describe in detail what you saw during the lesson

4. Provide specific "This was successful!" feedback

5. Provide specific "Here's what I'd like you to work on" feedback

6. Ask the teacher to reflect on your feedback

7. Choose a next step action and time commitment together

Did you faint or grow weak when you read Step 5? If you did, we're going to change that. By the end of this chapter you're going to be the feedback master. And you'll see your coaching confidence grow at least ten fold – I promise!

Let's unpack each of these sections, through a series of mini-scripts, so that you have a very clear picture of what to expect at each phase of the debriefing.

Restate the purpose for the coaching interaction (1 minute)

Hi Will! I'm so excited to meet with you to discuss yesterday's lesson. Remember that during our pre-conference we decided that it would be important for you to get some feedback on the number of student responses that you get when you ask the whole class to take an action. The example you gave me is that, when you ask your students to use their note sheets to jot down two ideas from the text they've read, you're noticing only about 50 percent of your kids actually do that. So, I set out during my observation to gather some information on that for you.

NOTES: This first step is a very quick frame for how the conversation will go and I am establishing a focus for the debriefing. Notice that I make it about 'us,' not 'me.' Also, by quickly recapping the purpose of the work, I'm allaying any fears that I might have been collecting notes for another purpose.

Ask the teacher to reflect on the teaching (5 minutes)

So Will, tell me what you thought about the level of engagement during the time I was in there. What did you notice? If you had a chance to do this lesson again, would you change anything? What might you adjust for tomorrow's lesson, based upon the students' performance today?

NOTES: Notice that I am prompting Will to start talking and debriefing his own teaching. When you're first coaching a teacher, you might find that getting this part of the conversation going can be difficult. This doesn't mean that your coaching isn't working, it just gives you an indication that the teacher is still learning how to reflect on his own teaching. Learning to reflect is part of building capacity within an organization, so give it time to develop. If you find that it's really difficult for a teacher to reflect on the spot, then leave a little note card on their desk as you leave the observation and ask them to jot down two things that were successful and two things that they might adjust. Then they bring the card full of their ideas and you can use it to jump-start the conversation.

A sticky situation that most coaches experience is when you ask a teacher how they think the lesson went and they say, "Fine." My go-to follow up question for a single word or single sentence reflection is this: tell me what was fine about the lesson. You can also say this: "Walk me through your lessons and tell me what I should have seen you doing and what I should have seen the kids doing at specific points." Just because you have to draw information out of teacher, doesn't mean that coaching isn't working.

In this type of scenario, it is tempting for me to just jump in and start talking…and talking…and talking! But I encourage you to avoid that knee-jerk reaction. Instead, tell yourself to work through any awkwardness or lack of reflection from the teacher. If you fail to teach a teacher how to reflect, then you are failing to build capacity for he or she to be able to self-evaluate their performance. After all, that's what coaching is all about: teaching the teachers to be reflective and critical of their own teaching, so that they are able to self-assess and make adjustments for greater instructional impact in the future.

Here are some additional questions you might ask during your debriefing:

- How do you think the lesson went?

- What would you do differently? Why?

- What triggered that thought?

- Were there specific students that you were particularly focused on?

- How is this different from how you might have delivered the lesson?

- Tell me what you thought when…

- How do you know that…?

- What I hear you saying is…

- What data or information do you have to support that?

- What did you want me to see you doing during this lesson?

- What did you want me to see your students doing during this lesson?

- What were you surprised about?

- What can you imagine us focusing on next?

- This leads me to think that we should take a look at…

Gut Check!

What three of the above sentence starters seem like they'd work for you? Coaching is about choosing several "go-to" phrases that you can count on working in almost every coaching scenario. Choose your three now!

Here's a big tip: *You must listen very carefully! Many times the teacher will slip in the very thing that you'd like to have them adjust during their next lesson right into the conversation.* If you find that a teacher says, "Well, you know I realize that my student desk arrangement isn't lending itself to lots of engagement with my kids," and that was your exact recommendation or next step, then go there right now! Oftentimes I'll say to a teacher (skipping the other parts of the debriefing), "You know, it's interesting that you mention that. I was going to suggest that we look at how we can turn the desks during your discussion times so that the students are able to literally look at each other and know who is going to ask the next question. I agree that this small change might have a really positive impact on the level of discussion and engagement during your text reading. When would you like to try that?" In that moment, I've just skipped over all of the other steps of the debrief because the teacher solved his own problem. And that's a great thing! You want to look for opportunities and little blips in the debriefing where teachers are solving their own problems, and then help them get those solutions into place.

I encourage you to use a structure of debriefing so that you can rely on that structure and focus on the conversation. But I caution that by always thinking about what you're going to say next, you may miss major leaps in the conversation.

Using your notes, describe in detail what you saw during the lesson (5 minutes)

This is where your knowledge of how to take notes is going to make a huge difference. Our next chapter will help you perfect the art of note-taking.

First off, when we do take notes in a classroom, we are jotting down what we saw, not what we thought. When I write down what I saw, that is not evaluative. When I write down what I thought, that is evaluative. I am going to ask you to get rid of one statement right now: *"I like (blank)…"* For example, "I liked it when you asked the students to restate their responses using complete sentences," or "I like it when you have the students use their jot sheet to take notes throughout the lesson." Ironically, so many coaches are afraid of being evaluative during their coaching, yet they use the "I like" statements all throughout!

Coaches should replace "I like" with "I saw" or "I noticed." What that does is change the conversation from evaluating the teaching according to what you think is good, bad or ugly and turns it into a sharing of facts. So, you might flip the "I like" statements like this:

Old: "I like how you asked the kids to turn to their partners and share their responses."

New: *"I noticed that you had the kids turn to their partners after every question you posed. I saw that 95 percent of your students were engaged with their partner during that time."*

Old: "I like when you ask the students to extend their answers to more complex sentences."

New: *"I see that your practice of requiring your students to use compound, complex answers to your questions is really paying off. Nearly all of your students' responses were complex."*

Old: "I like how you paced the lesson – it was fast enough that you didn't lose the kids, but slow enough that you didn't leave your struggling kids behind."

New: *"Your pacing really allowed for all kids to engage in the content. As I was looking at Student A (a struggling student), I noticed that she was able to complete the tasks along with the other kids."*

I have a quick tip for you: keep your notes in between you and the teacher during this segment of the debriefing. Why? Because you can use this opportunity to communicate that you are not judging, conducting a formal evaluation or writing anything scary or evaluative. I also try to make it a habit of pointing to my notes as I'm talking through what I saw. An example of this is: "You know, right here in my notes [pointing to notes and letting the teacher read it] I jotted down that you asked ten questions and Sarah answered the questions aloud a total of six times. I was wondering how we can mix it up a bit and incorporate more kids. What do you think?" When you look at that statement, there is no evaluation involved. I've just stated a fact and have shown the teacher exactly what I wrote in my notes. There's a little magic in that, trust me.

Gut Check!

What part of the debriefing process so far will be your biggest challenge? Name two teachers right now that you can practice the debriefing on. Practice makes perfect...even in coaching!

Provide specific "This was successful!" feedback (2 minutes)

There is an art to giving positive feedback and here's the formula for it:

positive feedback + data = change in practice

Here's an example of data-driven feedback: I am debriefing Sally Jo and she's done an absolutely fantastic job of getting her kindergarten kids to answer on signal during her phonemic awareness portion of the lesson. A typical debrief of a great lesson might go something like this:

Coach: *"Sally Jo, your lesson was so awesome! Great job!"*

Sally Jo: *"Thanks!"*

Coach: *"Keep it up!"*

Sally Jo: *"I will!"*

End of conversation.

I've told Sally Jo that she's done a great job, but I failed to provide data as to why that was a good job. So, here's how I add the data to that conversation and reinforce the 'why' behind her continuing to teach in this way:

Coach: *"Sally Jo, you literally had every single one of your kids answering on cue by giving your signal for wait-time and then giving the cue for their response! That meant that 100 percent of your kids got 100 percent of the practice on those ten blending words. Woo hoo!"*

Sally Jo: *"Thanks!"*

Coach: *"I want to tell you why it's so important that you continue to work to get 100 percent response. When we give kids as many opportunities to respond and receive feedback on a skill, they are more likely to master that skill. You provided every student in your classroom with ten practice opportunities today. Wow, I'll bet your mastery rate really skyrockets."*

Sally Jo: *"Ok, I'll keep it up!"*

What I've done with this approach is two-fold.

1. I've avoided the "I like" statement – even positive feedback must be data driven.

2. I've given Sally Jo the reasons why her practice was effective and why she needs to continue that particular practice.

It's funny, when I observe a debriefing where the coach is flowery with praise, I find the teacher has no clue what to do next, even though it's positive. If a coach says, "Oh Mark, you teach with such enthusiasm. Keep it up!" Mark is left wondering, "What about my teaching was enthusiastic and what exactly should I be keeping up?" I've had the opportunity to talk with teachers who have participated in really positive debriefings and ask them, "So, what are you supposed to do next?" More often than not, they say, "I'm not quite sure!"

When I re-frame my feedback this way: "Mark you are such an enthusiastic teacher! Your enthusiasm is contagious! Here are several examples of how your enthusiasm supports your kids learning more content," I've now given Mark specifics as to what to continue doing. Teachers need encouragement and data to support their positive teaching habits as well as the ones we are trying to alter. Data supports both corrective feedback and encouragement.

Before we jump into the framework for instructional conversations and debriefing, I want to give a quick note to you on the amount of time the coaching should take. One thing I notice is that coaches tend to spend too long on each coaching interaction because they are trying to make each moment incredibly meaningful and impactful. The problem is, when we spend too much time on our coaching interactions, we wear our teachers out.

I have a rule of thumb when I coach: I would rather have much shorter coaching interactions, but have them more often. I also want to be respectful that while coaching is my number one priority, my teachers have about a zillion other priorities that rate above coaching sessions with me. So, I try to organize the coaching interactions to be brief, insightful, action-based...and often!

Take a look at how you can organize the instructional debriefing to maximize your results.

Provide specific "Here's what I'd like you to work on" feedback (5 minutes)

It's very important that we set aside the fear that if I give direct feedback to teachers on their teaching, they will feel evaluated. I give you permission to let that go. Right now. C'mon. It's time.

You must feel lighter now!

What I hope that you're noticing is that by establishing the habit of providing data-driven, objective feedback to teachers from the top of the debriefing, when we come down to delivering the change items, your teachers are prepared. Here is an example:

> *"Court, I have two suggestions for you about how you can increase the retention on the vocabulary words that you're teaching, since we have identified that as a concern. What I'd like you to try is to limit your vocabulary list to five words. I know that it's hard to cut down your list, but I see that your students are really struggling to get the ten words mastered.*
>
> *The second suggestion is to then take more time teaching those five words. I saw a teacher recently take five steps with the words*

during her teaching: read the word and have the kids repeat it, give the full definition, give a student-friendly definition, give three examples of how the word describes a situation and then give three non-examples. I saw this as really effective in getting kids to master the use of those words. How do you think that will work for you?"

I want you to avoid making apologies for giving feedback. If you aren't providing feedback, then there is little purpose to the work. You will need to practice debriefing, and this particular step in the debriefing, so that it feels natural. Trust me, your teachers are looking at you to see how confident you feel giving this feedback. If they feel that you are soft-selling or apologetic about giving the feedback, they will not respect it. Be emboldened by the data you have collected and avoid being wishy-washy. Guts are mandatory here!

You see, here's where our feedback feels evaluative: when it comes out of thin air. When I link my corrective feedback and suggestions to the pre-conference and note-taking, then giving the teacher the "to do" during the debriefing seems much more natural and follows a logical flow. In fact, I suggest that you share the form for debriefing with your staff so that they know what to expect. When we keep the debriefing a mystery it just screams "I'm being evaluated!"

My hope is that by now you're seeing a trend: When we fail to explain the why and the how of coaching to teachers, we leave unnecessary room for interpretation. Not all of your teachers will love to be coached, but will hopefully be less resistant when you fully explain the coaching role and form to them. The more information that we can give to teachers, the less resistance we will create. I've seen whole coaching programs turn around when the coach goes to the teachers and says, "I know that coaching with me might not be your highest priority, but it is the main vehicle we are using to increase our scores. Since we are both charged by our principal to meet regularly for coaching, I'd like to show you what that looks like." Likewise, if you're feeling resistance to coaching, ask yourself, "Have I made assumptions that my teachers understand what coaching will look like?" The antidote to resistance is often found in your answer to that question.

Ask the teacher to reflect on your feedback (2 minutes)

After you have explained what you'd like the teacher to change, incorporate or adjust, I'd like you to follow through with a very simple question: "How do you think implementing _____ will impact the effectiveness of your teaching?"

You are not asking the teachers their opinion of your suggestions, you're asking them to reflect on its impact. Another important follow-up question is: "How can I support you in implementing this adjustment?" Notice that I'm not asking if they'll implement, I'm talking as if they've already agreed to it. If you've completely walked through the debriefing steps prior to this, you will find that having the teacher commit to actually doing something is very natural. In fact, teachers expect to have to do something! I've talked to so many teachers who have said, "I don't know why my coach doesn't tell me what to do," when the coach fails to close the deal.

And that's what this really is: closing the deal.

There might be a point where a teacher disagrees with you. Don't panic! If a teacher that I was coaching were to say, "I don't think that this will impact my teaching in any way because…," I would just turn the conversation to, "Ok, let's talk about what then would make a difference – what might you try, based upon the feedback that I've given you?" I keep the conversation in 'doing' mode. I don't back away, but I allow room for the teachers' opinion, while not losing the momentum.

Choose a next step action and time commitment together (1 minute)

This is really the step that all coaches should use to judge the value of their coaching: the commitment.

> *"So Court, you agreed to try cutting your vocabulary list in half so that you can spend more time directly teaching five of the words. I want to support you in implementing this change. What if I met with you next Tuesday during your prep time and together we could prepare your vocabulary list and lessons for the following week? This would help me get even better at doing this, too! I'm thinking that if we took twenty minutes during your prep, we could power through this. Does that work for you?"*

My conversation with Court could also sound like this:

> *"Court, when would be a good time to come in and see you teach the vocabulary words like we discussed? I would like to come in and collect some baseline data so that we can gauge the effectiveness of this new vocabulary strategy. Would Monday at 8:45 work for you?"*

If you want to ask a more open-ended question that will lead to action, you could try: *"Court, so in light of this information, what will tomorrow look like for you?"*

That leads Court down the path of altering something, but allows room for her to decide where she might make adjustments.

NOTES: I am moving my coaching into action right here. Without committing to actually doing something, we have just wasted time talking about the teaching. And we know from traditional professional development, that just talking about teaching doesn't change the quality of teaching. What you want to get from this step in the debriefing are three things:

1. What the teacher will try

2. When the teacher will try it

3. When you can get back to work with the teacher or see the new action in practice

If I have a teacher that says, "Yes, I'll try it," but does not commit to when, I know that unless I nail down a specific time, that suggested practice is not likely to make it into the regular teaching lesson. If you leave a coaching interaction with no follow-up action, not only will nothing change for the kids, the teacher will feel like coaching is a waste of time.

I usually pop a Post-It note into the teachers' box a couple of days after the debriefing and say, "Can't wait to see you on Tuesday at 8:45 a.m. for vocabulary. Have a great week!" That follow-up confirmation has served as a great reminder to teachers who leave the coaching room and forget to implement the to-do, and it also confirms that I will be following up.

Remember how in previous chapters I said that you should only have to start the coaching process (via the one-legged interview and open-ended concerns statement) once? Here's why: when you are following up with a teacher on something that they said they'd try, you're now cycling right back to the first phase of coaching: pre-conference! Essentially, as I talk to Court (from our example above) about when to come and see the vocabulary work, I'm already having that pre-conference. The coaching is now naturally flowing from phase to phase over and over again. That's how you'll know you've arrived.

The final step in the debriefing process is one that I encourage you to take once a month or once every two months: debriefing the coaching relationship. You may choose to ask these questions at the tail end of a coaching session or separate from the coaching:

- How can we improve upon our coaching exchanges in the future?

- What type of coaching technique might be even more supportive of you?

- Is there a time to debrief that would work better for you?

- What information and support do you need from me that you are not getting?

- What information and support that I give is helpful to you?

As we know, relationship in coaching is essential to digging in and getting the important instructional work done. You have to use your best judgment on how often to ask these questions, but your openness in receiving feedback yourself will only strengthen your relationships and ensure that your coaching has direct impact on the quality of the teacher's instruction.

Connect Your Coaching to the Common Core

One of the great benefits we have through the implementation of the Common Core is to re-evaluate what is working and what isn't working for us in the classrooms. I see it as a huge opportunity for each and every teacher to calibrate their teaching practices. One of the most important and significant aspects of the Core Standards is that each Standard not only tells us what to teach, but tells us how to teach it. This is a huge shift from regular standards, which focused mainly on what content the kids should learn.

Take advantage of this shift in practice by not only discussing what new and improved content we need to incorporate into our curriculum, but what instructional techniques and delivery adjustments we need to make. Pull cross-grade level groups together to identify the instructional practices that should be present in multiple classrooms and multiple grade levels. Use the "common" part of the Common Core to your coaching advantage!

Coaching Through Those Sticky Situations

Facebook fan, Jennifer B. asks: *How many "golden nuggets" should you leave a teacher with so they feel like they can move forward and not be overwhelmed?*

This is a great question because I feel like the answer will ultimately help coaches become more powerful without having to do much. In fact, this question is about doing less and getting bigger results.

The simplest, yet most annoying, answer is: as many as the teacher can handle. I know, super annoying that I don't give you a number. People like when I give hard and fast numbers, but it's not always that easy!

Really what I want coaches to ask themselves is this: what are 1-2 very concrete actions that I want this teacher to take so that we can get a noticeable change in student response? I want you to grab your highlighter and highlight the word "noticeable" in that sentence. Once you get a teacher to try even one thing that they can actually see at work in their classroom, then you have 'em hooked. In other words, they try one simple, but powerfully noticeable thing in their classroom, and then the next time, you can give them a couple of things to try because you have some momentum.

One of the biggest mistakes that I see coaches make is that they go too big with their recommendations and teachers are unable to see the effect of the action.

When you keep your recommendations short and sweet, a teacher can say, "Wow, I tried what you suggested and I saw a difference!" You now can fast-track the recommendations and increase the number of suggestions in future coaching interactions.

Permission and Preparation: The Dynamic Duo

Originally appeared on www.jackson-consulting.com,
June 6, 2013

I was working this week with a great group of super energetic leaders. We were getting organized on the Common Core (shocker!). One of the things that dawned on me during our work together was this: sometimes when you want people to make a change, you have to give them permission to make that change.

Let me explain.

For so long we've locked educators into, say, a certain way of delivering their content. (A statement like "I have to 'get through' all of the chapters by the end of the trimester" is one example that comes to mind). While it's become their habit, it also probably sticks in their minds as "the way we have to do things."

I remember telling a teacher that she no longer had to do the handwriting program each day (she had done it for 15 years, since the district had adopted daily videos for handwriting instruction), and she said, "Since when?"

The principal said, "Oh, we haven't done that for four years."

Her response? "No one ever told ME!"

It was funny, but also a bit frightening when you really think about it!

She needed the permission to stop doing something that had previously been required. I think we make too many assumptions that teachers know that they don't have to do certain things anymore – but they didn't quite catch our drift or remember the memo! We need to be explicit and explain:

1. What they need to stop and why

2. What they need to replace it with and why

So, in the handwriting teacher example, the principal said, "Sally, we are discontinuing our daily handwriting practice videos starting right now, but we are replacing that with differentiated instruction for reading so that we can increase our target teaching in reading by 15 minutes daily."

Now THAT'S clear!

Then, when we give folks permission to stop a certain practice, we must, must, must give them time and support in planning an alternative!

Oftentimes, we ask our teachers to make a change, but we forget that just informing them of the decisions (or new "thing") doesn't mean that they are able to incorporate that new thing right away. We have to give permission, and then support as they plan.

So, the follow up to the handwriting teacher example would be, "So, I've asked our coach, Jennie, to work with your grade level during your next two team meetings to help you get up and running on your differentiated plans – the data, the teaching and the grouping."

Permission.

Planning.

Step 4: Get to the Heart of Teaching and Learning

Think P.I.G. - that's my motto. P stands for Persistence, I stands for Integrity, and G stands for Guts.
~Linda Chandler

One of my jobs in supporting schools is to work with the principal and coach on what to look for when they are coaching teachers and gathering data during phase two of the coaching process. When I am teaching them how to collect data while they're observing, I always give the same directive: write everything down.

They nod, and we head into the first classroom.

The second I sit down in a classroom, I start writing. I jot down what the teacher is doing, I jot down what the kids are doing, I jot down what the assignment on the board says, I jot down how long certain tasks are taking, I jot down how many open-ended questions the teacher is asking the kids, I jot down who answers which questions. I literally jot everything down…I never stop!

It is inevitable that when I take a breath during my note-taking, I look over to the coach and principal and they have, at most, two bullet points of notes. And they look at me and one of them will whisper, "What on earth are you writing down?"

And I say, "Everything!"

I have learned through many years of observing teaching that the more I write down, the better my debriefing will go. More information equals a stronger debriefing. Also, more information means that I'm likely to be able to pick up on a pattern of behaviors that I might want to address. For example, I remember visiting a classroom once where the teacher called on the same student 17 times in ten minutes, while the other kids did not even answer once. I was able to say, during the debriefing, "Were you aware that you called on Kevin 17 times in the ten minutes I was in your classroom, and that the other students did not answer during that time? What effect do you think that has on their skill mastery? How might we adjust the routine so that all kids have the opportunity to respond and receive feedback from you?"

Without the data that I had gathered during my observation, my debriefing might have sounded like this, "You know, you called on Kevin a lot. I'd like to talk about how you can call on other kids more often. What do you think?" When I fail to gather enough data through my note-taking during an observation, I end up giving very vague and often evaluative data such as, "I really liked your lesson," or "I think you should increase the level of engagement to get kids more engaged." We need to make the connection that the amount of data that we collect during an observation is linked to the quality of the debriefing with that teacher.

In preparing to go into a class to observe, I think back to my pre-conference and ask myself, "What kind of data should I be picking up so that I can provide specific feedback to the teacher on our

---

Gut Check!

Stop and ask yourself this question: Could the kind of feedback that I am giving to teachers actually be causing resistance? What are some possible examples of this in my coaching?

---

focus area during this cycle of coaching?" If, for example, I'm working with a teacher on increasing engagement during his lessons so that more kids are doing more work, then I want to capture how many required responses the teacher gave in a particular period of time. If I am supporting a teacher in increasing discussion during comprehension instruction, then I want to grab as much information as I can on the type of questions posed to the kids, the wait-time or think-time the teacher gives prior to opening the discussion, the names of the kids most involved in the discussion, and what the kids who are not involved in the discussion are doing. I find that folks typically head into the classroom to gather data before they've analyzed exactly what kind of data they need to pick up in order to have a strong and helpful debriefing.

When I can provide teachers with very specific feedback, then they have a very clear problem to solve. Here is an example: I go into Holly's classroom because we have agreed that she will work on implementing a new wait-time signal to let kids know that they should not be blurting out answers, but rather taking time to think about what they say before they answer. So, we established during the pre-conference that I will take notes on three things:

1. How many blurted, off-signal answers there are?

2. How much wait-time is Holly giving before she has students answer?

3. Which kids are answering the questions/which kids she is calling on?

I decide to set up my note-taking page this way:

Question	Wait-time	Blurters	Responses/By Whom

In the first column, I will write each question that Holly poses in a different row under the header "Question." Then in the wait-time column I will write the number of seconds (I will use the second hand on my watch to be exact) Holly waited before accepting an answer. I will put a tally in the column "Blurters" if someone blurts out – if I can catch their name in that column, even better! And then I will jot down the responses that the kids had and write who was responsible for answering that question in the final column.

When I sit down to debrief Holly, I will give her actual numbers from the columns. I might find that Holly asked six questions while I was observing and each time she averaged between five and fifteen seconds of wait-time before she called on a student to respond. There were five blurts...and they were done by the same two students, Sam and Jacqueline.

So as I share this data with Holly, her mission is very clear:

- To increase her wait time from five seconds to a minimum of twenty seconds for extended response questions

- To talk with Sam and Jacqueline about managing their blurting and give them alternatives and consequences for continuing to blurt out answers

Now let's imagine that I hadn't taken data-based notes. I went into Holly's classroom and I found that kids blurted and her wait time fluctuated quite a bit. My debriefing might have gone something like this: "Holly, one thing I really want you to work on is giving more wait time. I also want you to work on getting a handle on the blurting." That is so vague! And it's likely to lead to little action – not because the teacher is resistant, but because the teacher has no idea what I'm suggesting!

To get you jump-started in your note-taking and observations, here is a short list of the types of measureable elements of teaching that you can look for during an observation. By the way, this list of "look fors" in the classroom relate back to our first chapter on context and content of instruction.

Here is a short list of the type of data I will typically gather during an observation:

- Number of whole group/individual responses

- Number of responses from particular students (GATE, Special Ed, ELL, intensive or strategic student)

- Quality of responses (complete thoughts, extended responses, use of academic language)

- Objective or purpose of the activity is totally observable and matches the task in which students are engaging

- Perfect practice/number of corrections

- Amount of feedback/quality of feedback

- Evidence of the explicit teaching model: teach, model, practice, feedback, apply, feedback, assess

- How students are grouped for small group work

- The number of actual instructional minutes versus scheduled instructional minutes

- Quality of discussion of text: on topic, partially on topic, off topic, fully on topic

- Timing or pacing of particular parts of a lesson

- Quality of questions (Recall only? Deeper thinking questions?)

- Rate of wait-time

- Teacher talk vs. student action

- Teacher using and teaching academic language

Gut Check!

Are you stuck in a rut during your observations? Which three types of data from the list above would help boost the effectiveness of your coaching? Which particular teachers' names come to mind when you think about measuring these three items?

I am not a fan of using checklists to take notes during observations because I find them more limiting than useful. Most checklists, by nature, are set up to have you check in a box that you have seen a particular piece of instruction or technique in action during your observation. What we know about instruction is that quality teaching habits that result in kids mastering the content do not happen once in a lesson, they take place again and again throughout the lesson. Most checklists are not set up to measure the *quality* of the teaching, but are designed to measure the presence of a particular technique or strategy. If I am required to use a checklist, here's my approach:

1. I set up my note-taking sheet on a blank sheet of paper, based upon the data that we want to collect for the debriefing

2. I take my notes as I usually would, as if I weren't using the checklist

3. Once the observation is done, I highlight on my notes the instruction that is related to the items on the checklist that I was using

4. I end up with the best of both worlds: data to complete the checklist and quality-based data collected outside of the checklist

I've learned the value of remembering to ask the students what they are working on during an observation. It is so common that we spend all of our time looking at the teacher, we sometimes forget to measure the effect of the instruction on the kids. So, some questions I regularly ask the kids are:

- What are you working on right now?

- How will you know you are finished with the assignment?

- What do you have to do to get an 'A' on this assignment?

- What is the objective of the lesson?

- What do you do if you don't understand part of your assignment?

- How much time do you have to complete this?

There are two types of evidence that any observer can pick up during a classroom observation:

1. Big picture evidence

2. Nitty-gritty evidence

Big picture evidence definitely provides me a picture of what is going on in the classroom, but the picture is so broad, there is little coaching impact if I were to share it. Big picture evidence also leaves a very wide path for interpretation, and interpretation leads to evaluation in so many cases, so coaches will want to avoid this type of evidence-collecting. Here are several examples of big picture evidence:

- There are 18 girls and 14 boys in the class

- The class began at 2:17 p.m.

- The objective for the lesson is to learn the life cycle

- The teacher checked for understanding quite a bit

Nitty-gritty evidence will give me information on the nuances of the instruction and, most importantly, helps guide me to a very specific debriefing with the teacher. The nitty-gritty evidence is focused on the "cause and effect" relationship between the teacher and the students, and highlights for the teacher exactly the outcome of the instructional strategies or lesson design during a short period of observation. Here are examples of nitty-gritty evidence:

- The teacher asked five open-ended questions and 85 percent of the students logged responses into their think journals

- During the math instruction, four students sat with their hands raised for a minimum of three minutes each, waiting for the teacher to repeat the directions

- During my 15-minute observation in the classroom, the teacher redirected Jonathan's behavior seven times. Five redirections were for slamming his desk shut and two redirections were for turning his back to the teacher during the instruction

- The teacher visited the below-benchmark students three times to gauge their level of understanding of the content

Let me give you two scenarios to analyze:

Scenario 1: We just left Shonda's class and have taken many notes on her reading lesson. When we pull her in for a debriefing, the coach says, "Shonda, we noticed that you were struggling to keep the kids engaged in your classroom during reading." Shonda nods in agreement. "As we were preparing for the debriefing, we realized that the best way to combat the low engagement is to increase the pacing of the lesson – make the lesson move faster. The goal of this is to avoid any lulls in teaching that might provide students an opportunity to check out or misbehave. Does that make sense?" Shonda says, "Yes, that makes perfect sense. I'm really struggling to keep the kids interested." Shonda leaves.

Later that day, I run into Shonda and I say, "Shonda I'm not quite sure that if I had received the feedback that you did about increasing engagement that I would know what to do with that information tomorrow as I teach. What do you think?" She says, "That's absolutely true! I get the idea of what my coach wants me to do, but I don't know how to do it."

So, Shonda understood conceptually that she needed to increase her pace so that she can keep more kids on track and engaged, but she is missing the "how" part of getting it done. This is an example of what happens when big picture evidence is presented. Even teachers who are motivated to improve their performance and skill are missing the proper tools and feedback to be able to improve!

Scenario 2: We just left Shonda's class and have taken notes about the levels of engagement in her class. During the pre-conference, we had determined with Shonda that she is having a lot of disruptive behaviors crop up and she feels that her pacing is too slow, which gives kids too much time to fool around during her lessons. We set up a T-chart to capture the notes. The left side of the T-chart had the minutes that we were in the classroom listed (from 1-10, as we were in her class from 9:10 to 9:20 a.m.). The right side of the T-chart was an account of what the students and Shonda were doing during each minute of observation.

When we gather for the debriefing, we show Shonda our notes and let her know that she lost the momentum and the engagement of the students in the sixth minute of instruction when she had to re-direct one of her talkative girls three times. Shonda said, "Oh my, I didn't realize that I had to redirect her three times, it seemed like only one time!" As we shared the rest of the notes, she realized that her pacing slowed down because of outside distractions: kids wanting to get a drink, a request from the office to send a child home early, and her redirections of Cecily for talking to her partner during the lesson.

Before Shonda left, we outlined two steps for her to take to limit the distractions and increase her lesson pacing:

1. She would establish a consequence for students asking to use the restroom or getting a drink during instruction and she would enforce this liberally

2. She would talk directly with Cecily about her talking issue and develop a signal that would put Cecily on notice to watch her behavior long before it becomes an issue

We made an appointment to get back into Shonda's room within one week to check on her progress.

What Scenario 2 provided that Scenario 1 did not, was clarity of action. There was no question as to what Shonda needed to do when she got back to her classroom, plus, she would be very certain that she was following through on the coach's recommendations because they were so clear. This, no doubt, would end in a positive coaching cycle for Shonda if she followed through.

Coaches will often say to me, "You make coaching look so easy!" but the reality is, I've been practicing it for years. There were many times early in my coaching career that I wrote down all of the wrong things, and I learned the hard way when the debriefing was painful! I can think back to many times where I gave the most horrible, big picture feedback that, no doubt, left teachers thinking, "huh?" But the more I coach, the clearer I am on what it takes to give very specific advice – and how to collect the notes to be able to give that advice. Collecting evidence is a skill that needs major practice. Why not start now?

Obviously, nitty-gritty evidence is the type of evidence that leads to a very powerful debriefing because there is not much room for interpretation – and that's a good thing when you're steering clear of evaluation. Nitty-gritty evidence also allows you to measure the level of implementation by the teacher. Learning to collect nitty-gritty evidence takes time, but it is one of the big keys to successful coaching. In fact, I find that the debriefings are so much smoother because I can rely so heavily on my notes.

Connect Your Coaching to the Common Core

Remember that as you are observing and debriefing your teachers as they implement the Common Core Standards, their success is not built on whether they teach the Standards. Their success (and that of their students) is built on whether they teach the Standards at the right level of complexity.

For example, if the Standard says that the teacher must teach students how to analyze the key ideas and details of a piece of informational text, you must be looking for analysis of the key ideas and details. You might see the students identifying the key ideas and details of the text, but if they are not doing analysis of key ideas and details during the lesson, the level of complexity of the teaching is off. Know your standards and their complexity.

Coaching Through Those Sticky Situations

Facebook fan, Ann J. asks: *What do you say to the teachers who think they don't need your help?*

This goes back to our very first chapter on making sure that there is instructional focus set clearly and cleanly by the principal. If I am working with a teacher that says, "I don't need your help," (and trust me that's happened many, many times!), I say something like, "You know, I understand that it's really weird to have a coach come into your classroom – I admit that it's sometimes odd for me too! However, Mrs. Thompson, our principal, has set the expectation that we all need coaching. What I'd like to do to make this as smooth as possible is to set up an appointment next where I can come in and chat with you about your lesson planning for next week. What times work best for you?"

The goal here is not to dwell on whether or not you're going to coach that person, but to move the conversation swiftly to *when* you're going to coach that person. I find that this takes practice, but when you become more confident in this kind of conversation (and, by the way, the only way to become more confident is to just do more of it!), you'll find that you are more willing to talk with teachers who are resistant to your coaching.

I promise it gets easier!

What Exactly Should I Be Looking for During a Class Observation?

Originally appeared on www.jackson-consulting.com,
November 29, 2012

Class observation by a coach or principal strikes fear in the hearts of many teachers and I know exactly why! Who wants to be judged? Worse yet, who wants to be judged by someone who hasn't likely been in the classroom for years, and was on their cell phone during the professional development sessions?

Um. Not me!

Principals and coaches – we owe it to our staff to be more proactive, less scary and lurker-ish during our observations.

Let me explain.

First of all, you have to have a focus for the instructional work you're doing on your campus. This is the PURPOSE behind your observations. When teachers know that "the principal is looking for increased engagement levels from my ELL students during ELA instruction," then two cool things happen:

1. They tend to focus on integrating that work/technique/strategy more broadly and deeply into their everyday teaching because they know that you'll be around to look for it. This is a big motivator for a lot of teachers.

2. Their anxiety lessens because they realize that they actually have a chance to meet our expectations because our expectations aren't random, they're focused.

When we have no instructional focus at the school site, then our observations (whether it's true or not) seem like a "gotcha" – and that's not a motivation that will sustain long-term growth in any staff.

Implementation due to fear is not a recommended tactic!

So, principals and coaches, you should start with a focus and let your staff know that you will be in their classrooms formally and on a drop-in basis, looking for the instructional focus in action at any time of the day.

Secondly, when you go into classrooms, you should approach it as a balcony-sitter at a theater production.

Huh?

Let me explain.

When you sit in the balcony, you have perspective. You can see the other audience members, you can see the orchestra, you can see the entire width of the stage. Sometimes you can even see into the wings of the stage and see the actors' entrances and exits.

When the actors are on stage or the audience is situated really close to the stage, there is so much perspective lost. This is the teacher's position – the teacher is so close to the action and right in the middle of it most of the time, it's hard to gain perspective and hard to evaluate the full orchestration of the lesson.

(Some might argue that when you sit close you have tremendous focus, but this doesn't necessarily serve our immediate purpose during class observation!)

When you have a PERSPECTIVE mindset during classroom observations, here's what you should be looking for:

- How is the teacher orchestrating the lesson? Is it well orchestrated and smooth or choppy and disjointed? What is the evidence of this?

- What is the pacing like? Are the students keeping up with the lesson?

- Are the groupings benefiting the students? How do you know?

- Are particular students having trouble with the intensity of the lesson? Which students? How could you tell?

- When in the lesson did the teacher start to "lose" students? What did that look like? What did the students start to do that showed you that they were no longer focused on the lesson?

- What percentage of the time did the teacher spend in direct instruction? Guided practice? Application?

- How many re-directions (which don't have to be a bad thing!) did the teacher do during each portion of the lesson?

- What was the students' product? What did the teacher expect in terms of written response? Discussion or oral response? Did the students use complete sentences and extended thoughts during the lesson?

- Was it readily apparent what the goal of the lesson(s) was? Did the teacher revisit the goal to remind the kids? When you asked students what they were working on, could they explain the task and the purpose behind it?

You see, an observation (and the feedback given) won't be helpful at all unless it gives the teacher perspective that they cannot otherwise get when they're right in the trenches doing the teaching.

I start my informal and formal rounds by stating to myself the response to this question: *"What perspective do I want to give my teachers today that they wouldn't get if I didn't observe them?"*

Now THAT's purpose, folks!

Step 5: Get Some Thick Skin

Guts are a combination of confidence, courage, conviction, strength of character, stick-to-itiveness, pugnaciousness, backbone and intestinal fortitude. They are mandatory for anyone who wants to get to and stay at the top.

~D. A. Benton

At this point, I hope that you have picked up the idea that many times our lack of focus and direction in coaching can actually create resistance from those we coach. Oftentimes when I'm coaching a group of coaches, they list "resistance" as one of their biggest frustrations and the one thing that keeps them from getting into classrooms and coaching teachers. When we analyze where the resistance is coming from, we so often end up going all the way back to the beginning of the coaching role, and analyzing if the coaching role was set up properly. And do you know what we typically find?

The role of the coach wasn't clear from the very beginning.

The expectations of both the coach and teacher during coaching were not properly fleshed out. The coach was intimidated by the role and that kept her out of the classrooms. The longer the coach stayed out of the classrooms, the more the trust eroded. The more the trust eroded, fewer teachers were open to coaching and the resistance got out of hand. It's a vicious cycle. If you can relate to any of this, I want you to know that it is not too late to turn things around. You may be thinking, "Jill, I've been coaching for seven years. Of course there's no way to turn this resistance around now!"

Well, actually there is.

You just start from the beginning.

Yep. Chapter 1. Start by getting very focused on what coaching is and isn't.

I recently facilitated a pretty tough conversation between a principal, a coach and the staff about 'righting' the coaching ship. Before talking with the staff, the coach, principal and I scripted what they were going to say to the staff during their upcoming meeting and then practiced it many times. By the way, rehearsing is a great way to ensure that your more difficult debriefings go well – I highly recommend it!

Here was the basic outline of what the principal shared with the staff:

"Folks, I want to take a few minutes to talk about our coaching plan. First off, I want to acknowledge that I have done a pretty poor job in the past at setting up the coaching role. Our greatest asset on campus is our team of teachers, and in order to increase how well and how effectively we teach, we need to continue to hone our craft. This is where Bonnie comes in. Bonnie was hired as our coach three years ago. At first, I don't think any of us had a clue what to do with her! I know Bonnie would agree. When I first rolled out to you the idea that we were going to have a coach, I realized that some of you were less than excited, and instead of explaining what the coaching would look like, I assumed (incorrectly) that when Bonnie showed up, everyone would be on board.

So, her first few weeks she visited classes and got to know you and your kids a bit better. Soon after, we began pulling Bonnie from her coaching schedule to cover for teachers when we couldn't find subs – I remember even asking her to cover the phones when we were short on office staff. Obviously, this is not what the role of the coach is designed for. The longer time went on, the more Bonnie would try to get into your classrooms, but it was difficult for her because it appeared that you were not open to coaching. Let me be very clear: I am not surprised that you appeared disinterested or resistant to the coaching. After all, I gave you absolutely no context for what was expected of you and Bonnie. I want to apologize to you all for not structuring the coaching more clearly.

So I ask you to allow me to hit the 'reset' button on our coaching process. Our scores have shown that we are doing a lot of things really well for our kids instructionally. However, recent data has shown that our struggling students in reading and math are not reaching their growth targets. We are having difficulty moving that group of students. I see this as a very important focus area for our coaching from this point forward.

Over the next two staff meetings, I have asked Bonnie to share with you the role of the coach, the flow of the coaching, the timeline for coaching and what she sees as a logical place to start with each of you. Please know that I have asked and expect Bonnie to be working with each of you regularly. Some teachers might meet with Bonnie more often and some less often, but everyone on our campus will receive coaching from Bonnie. How you are coached will be up to Bonnie and you – she has a structure for how to do this.

I appreciate you taking all of this information into consideration, and allowing us to start fresh with our coaching work. We know that the most powerful form of professional development is coaching, and we want to be using our coach in ways that have the greatest impact. While coaching might not be easy and it might require additional time from you, it is a major tool that we will use to continue to improve our service to our kids."

Here are the highlights of that conversation:

- Acknowledging that the coaching role was not working

- Taking responsibility for a lack of support of the coaching role

- Re-committing to the coaching role in the purest form: as professional development

- Re-establishing the expectation that coaching is going to be a part of every teacher's ongoing professional development

- Committing to re-training folks on what coaching is and isn't

I was at the staff meeting where the principal shared this information and the response was interesting. It was almost as if the teachers were relieved that someone finally addressed the elephant in the room and acknowledged what everyone was thinking. A collective "whew!" was heard. When I talked with teachers after the staff meeting, so many of them were relieved that they were finally going to understand the coaching role better, and many admitted that they needed to adjust their attitudes and they welcomed a fresh start with Bonnie.

What's the lesson here? It's never too late for a re-do! The other lesson? Resistance always comes from somewhere – there is a root or source from which the resistance is springing. Here are possible sources of resistance. The good news is they're all fixable!

- Workload is overwhelming

- Poor experience with a past coach

- Lack of follow-through from the principal

- Gossipy staff

- Issues within the team that extend to coaching

- Relationship issues with the coach

- Lack of trust in the coach's ability to keep coaching private

- Lack of trust in the principal's ability to carry through with the implementation

- Lack of understanding of what is required of the teacher

- Miscommunication of expectations between the principal and coach

- General poor attitude toward change of any kind (by the way, these are the folks that you'll never change, so give yourself permission to let it go!)

The question is, if you are off course, are you and the principal committed to fixing it? Are you willing to have a conversation with the individuals or groups on your campus to set things up properly from here on out? I hope you'll have the guts to make coaching right. It's essential to the success of your teachers and kids.

> ### Gut Check!
>
> Ask yourself this: Am I in the habit of characterizing my entire staff as resistant, when the resistance lies with a few? Am I overlooking what is going well and over-generalizing what is not going well? What attitude cleanup do I personally need to do?

Ultimately, your coaching success rests on your ability to create and hone very specific coaching skills. Managing resistance is a skill, just like conducting a successful debriefing is a skill. As you build your resistance management skills, I want you to consider these ideas:

1. Just because you are experiencing resistance to coaching, does not mean that you're doing something wrong

2. If there is no resistance to coaching, then you are most likely not coaching teachers to make significant enough adjustments to their teaching

3. There is a difference between resistance and unprofessionalism

4. Make "keep going back" your coaching motto

Now, let's take a look at each of these ideas in depth:

Just because you are experiencing resistance to coaching, does not mean that you're doing something wrong.

Let's be real: coaching takes time. And lack of time is the number one complaint that teachers have in terms of getting their teaching jobs done. So, as a coach, the very nature of your role is to steal away a bit of the most precious, and hard to come by, thing on campus. Where I see coaches making a serious mistake is in their delivery of coaching. They beat around the bush or try to soft-sell the coaching content so much so that they're wasting teachers' time! For example, during a debriefing, the coach might say, "So, what do you think you ought to do to adjust the results of this lesson?" And the teacher comes up with some ideas that obviously are not along the lines of what the coach was thinking. Then the coach says, "Well, those are certainly some ideas. Can you think of others?" They go back and forth like this several times and I'm over in the corner watching this whole debacle and I want to shout out (and actually have several times), "Just tell him what you want him to do right now!"

Teachers appreciate a coach that can get to the point. It's a time saver. And for any teacher, saving time is crucial.

I want you to practice the art of thickening your skin and not taking everything so personally in your coaching work. You need to practice figuring out the difference between frustrated, overwhelmed and truly resistant. Frustrated is a teacher saying, "Ugh, I just feel like we grasp at straws around here! We go from one thing to another. Coaching just seems like a whole other quick-fix that we're trying. That makes me so mad!" Overwhelmed is, "I just can't take on anything else – especially coaching! I'm new to the grade level, I've gotten two new teammates since Spring Break, I've got two new ELL kids who just popped onto my class list and I have report cards due by Thursday at 3 p.m. I wish I could coach with you, but there is no way that I can!" And finally, true resistance: "I will not coach with you. After all, I've been teaching 15 years longer than you. What on earth could you help me with? You don't even know my kids!"

If I analyze the statements and tailor my approach, I can easily navigate my way through the resistance. Let's try it:

"Ugh, I just feel like we grasp at straws around here! We go from one thing to another. Coaching just seems like a whole other quick-fix that we're trying. That makes me so mad!"

- *Analysis:* This is a frustrated teacher who has been-there-done-that in terms of professional development. She probably feels like the district is committed to coaching for now, but will probably change direction quickly, so there's really no need to invest much in it. This teacher is obviously failing to see coaching as an opportunity to improve the scores in the classroom. Making a connection with this teacher and honestly discussing the lack of follow-through on previous "new things" is important. Pretending that these things didn't happen in the district will not solve the resistance, in fact, it will continue to add to it.

- *Action:* Avoid apologizing. It is not your job to defend coaching! I would set up a casual time to touch base with this teacher. I might say, "Hey Jane, I realized as we talked yesterday that you're really frustrated with coaching and how it seems like one more thing to do. Since both of us are required to coach and we can't get rid of each other just yet, let's set up a time to touch base every two weeks. I promise to keep our every-two-week meeting at no more than thirty minutes. How about I email you and set up a time for us to meet, at your convenience, next week?

"I just can't take on anything else – especially coaching! I'm new to the grade level, I've gotten two new teammates since Spring Break, I've got two new ELL kids who just popped onto my class list and I

have report cards due by Thursday at 3 p.m. I wish I could coach with you, but there is no way that I can!"

- *Analysis:* This teacher is just plain overwhelmed and, judging by the list of things on her plate, I don't blame her. The first order of business is to come along side her and help her prioritize a plan for getting everything done. This is a great opportunity to build a coaching connection with this teacher.

- *Action:* Set up a time right now to help this teacher get unstuck. When you meet with the teacher, support her by helping prioritize tasks and show where you might be of support in accomplishing her tasks. What I usually find is that these teachers have put too many things on their plates themselves and, as an outside observer, I can help take a few things off the "must-do-now" list.

"I will not coach with you. After all, I've been teaching 15 years longer than you. What on earth could you help me with? You don't even know my kids!"

- *Analysis:* Now this is a resistant teacher. This person is telling you that she will not work with you. And the tone of the response is rather rude. You have two choices: de-escalate the situation or escalate the situation to the principal level. I highly suggest that you try several times to get in and support this teacher before you move to involving the principal. In fact, some teachers, whether you like it or not, are going to see what you're made of and do so by testing you. While I don't encourage you to wage all out war with this teacher, visiting back with the teacher in a few days following this exchange does allow for the teacher to see that you're unafraid to try again. Most teachers will come around eventually.

- *Action:* Casually run into the teacher in the hallway a few days later and say, "You know, I understand that this coaching thing can be a bit awkward for both of us, but I'd like to talk to you about how we can work together on creating some opportunities with your struggling readers, Jose, Jeffrey, Tanya and Stacy. Can we talk during your prep time on Friday?" What you've done here is three-fold: you have acknowledged that coaching isn't working so well between you right now, you've given a very specific direction to head and then you've given a specific time to connect. If, after trying this approach 3-4 more times, the teacher still refuses to work with you, then it's time to go to the principal. But that is so rare.

Gut Check!

There is tremendous power in addressing the elephant in the room, and while people might cringe in the process, they will thank you later. It never fails! What are two "elephants in the room" that you need to directly discuss with a team or your staff? What is the purpose for a to-the-point discussion of these "elephants?"

One of the most valuable coaching skills to hone is your ability to not take things personally. And these types of scenarios will help you hone that skill and show teachers what you're worth as a coach. I always equate coaching to the flight attendant on the plane. As some-one who takes 2-4 flights almost each week, when there is turbulence or an oddly-acting passenger, the first thing I do is look at the flight attendant to see how he is reacting. If he sits down and straps in, I'm pretty sure we're going to crash. If he sits down, straps in and calls someone on the phone, I'm 100 percent positive that we're going to crash. If there's turbulence and he is calm and continues chatting to passengers and sips his coffee, I'm pretty sure we're going to be alright.

Coaching is the same way. Our staff members are constantly looking at us to see how we are reacting to particular situations. The overwhelmed teacher is watching us work steadily to help her get unstuck. The frustrated teacher is watching us to see if we're easily deterred from getting back into the coaching cycle after a bit of resistance. And the resistant teacher? Well, as much as I hate to admit it, that person is typically seeing if you have the guts to come back… and back…and back.

If there is no resistance to coaching, then you are most likely not coaching teachers to make significant enough adjustments to their teaching.

Just having a coach on campus does not mean that coaching is taking place. It's what the coach does that will determine the effectiveness of the coaching. If we are committed to improving the efficiency and effectiveness of teaching, to the degree that we can see the effect of coaching on student achievement, it means that teachers are going to have to make more than superficial changes to their teaching.

Let me tell you a little story about a school in the Midwest. The Superintendent of Schools called me in to support his district in raising their scores and helping them get out of district-wide school improvement. Only one out of their nine schools had made Adequate Yearly Progress (AYP). And even that one school made AYP through a loophole in the system. As I met with his leadership team, we realized that the main issue in making AYP and increasing their student performance was that the teachers lacked general care in preparing their lessons, and much of the instruction was of the "winging it" variety – made up on the spot. When I asked the principals if they'd done work to adjust this lack-of-planning issue, the general response was that they had done a lot of training in this area.

The school had worked with another training firm for two years on professional learning communities (PLCs). The principal said that they had worked to get teacher teams meeting regularly to plan instruction and work through their monthly data. He showed me the group norm posters, the rotating schedules of how the teams met with their instructional aides within their departments and across departments, and the report forms that each group created after they met. The principal said that the teachers loved the PLC process and "were getting lots out of it." I have to admit, it was a pretty well-organized system, but something was missing and I set up time to meet with the department teams to ask a few questions.

I met with each of the grade level teams and asked them these questions: What are PLCs, what is the purpose of the PLCs and what is a "good" PLC?

Each team described PLCs like this: "It's basically a department meeting." When I asked them the purpose of PLCs, without fail, the teams responded something like this: "PLCs are an opportunity for our team to meet and discuss what we're doing in the classroom." When I asked them what a good PLC was, unanimously they said, "A good PLC is one that finishes the agenda." My bonus question to each group was, "Do you benefit from your PLC work?" They all said that they really loved meeting in PLCs because it was basically what they were already doing before their PLC training.

Already doing that? Hmm…

You see here was the deal: everyone loved the PLC training because they didn't feel like they had to change much. They had missed the whole point! (By the way, this is not a commentary on PLC training or PLCs – I've seen healthy and productive PLCs as critical to the success of many districts and schools).

Then I realized something: the reason why they were so positive about the training, is because all they had to do was change the name of the meeting time from "Team Meeting" to "PLC" and they were done. Voila! No change in practice, no increased commitment, no expectation of more collaboration. No wonder they loved it so much!

That's called "new names for old practices syndrome" – we change the name and feel like we've really done something!

I hope that it gives you some comfort when I say this: If you are asking teachers to make legitimate adjustments to their teaching, then there will be discomfort.

Successful coaches really take that statement to heart and realize that discomfort is common – and a sign of implementation. In fact, I use resistance and lack of resistance as a measuring stick at times. While I am not looking to increase resistance or ask for more of it, I use it to help gauge the breaking-in period as we're implementing something new.

There is a difference between resistance and unprofessionalism.

I am going to make this section short and sweet because how you handle unprofessionalism really comes down to a gut check.

First off, any coach should be able to handle a fair amount of resistance. The big piece of advice that I can give is *keep going back.* Keep going back, especially in the face of resistance, so that teachers know that they can't scare you away and that you are committed to supporting them through it all. The second piece of advice that I can give is *don't take it so darn personally.* Stay away from defensiveness and feeling like any bit of resistance or frustration is directed entirely toward you. It's usually not. Give me an overly sensitive coach who takes things personally and I'll give you a coaching career that will be short-lived.

However, there are a very select handful of times that you will need to call in reinforcements or wave the white surrender flag.

There are times when a teacher's resistance crosses the line and their treatment of you becomes personally hurtful, embarrassing, attacking or publicly rude. It is in these cases that you need to bring the principal in to support you.

Here are some examples of resistant verses unprofessional:

Resistant: *"I hate this coaching thing. It's such a waste of time and I can't wait for us to move on to the next thing!"*

Unprofessional: *"I hate you! You didn't even get good results when you were a teacher, so I have no idea why you think you can tell me what to do."*

Resistant: *"I will meet with you, but I only have ten minutes because I have much more important things to do."*

Unprofessional: [Slams the door in the coach's face and locks it].

There will be a few times in a coach's career where he will be forced to go and talk with the principal about the unprofessionalism of a teacher. Here is how I would talk with my principal about the unprofessional teacher (NOTE: Use as little emotion in this conversation as possible – just state the facts):

"Mrs. Sweeney, I want to talk to you about my coaching relationship with Mr. Shipp. I have tried to follow your expectation by meeting regularly with each teacher. Everyone else is agreeing to meet with me except for Mr. Shipp. I have worked to engage him in different ways, to no avail. He has let it be known to me and his colleagues that he has no plans to receive coaching and my four attempts at working with him have proven just that: he is unwilling to be coached. At this point, I need your direction in determining whether Mr. Shipp is coachable by me or whether I should turn his coaching over to you."

If you find yourself having this conversation often, then it is likely that you need some work on thickening of the skin. I will say that most coaches that I work with will have two or three teachers like this throughout the course of their coaching career. I know that we learn to do difficult things by doing difficult things – and this extends to coaching, for sure. The more you deal with resistance, the better you get at dealing with resistance.

When I first began consulting, I would be a nervous wreck before I visited a client for the first time. I didn't know what to expect. It is not uncommon for me to be met with a less-than-excited reception! Of course, I can expect that because folks are told that they *have* to work with me. But what I've realized is that through the years I've built up the skills and toughness to be able to handle criticism, frustration, and all-out war on what I'm asking a district or school to do. I have learned that the best way to calm myself down when

I'm feeling particularly attacked is to repeat, "This is not personal, you didn't invent the concept of consultation!" I know it sounds silly, but if I keep repeating that phrase, I tend to take resistance less personally.

We have to practice the discipline of not taking things personally.

Make "keep going back" your coaching motto.

Perhaps the simplest, yet most important, idea that I will give you in this chapter is: *keep going back*. When the teachers are resistant, *keep going back*. When they blame you for the new program, *keep going back*. When they say that you have less experience than them and you can't possibly be of service, *keep going back*. When it feels like they're avoiding you, *keep going back*. When the teachers won't make eye contact with you during a team meeting, *keep going back*. When you walk into the teacher's lounge and everyone stops talking, *keep going back*.

I heard the pastor of my church speak on the ministry of "being there." He used the Reverend Jesse Jackson, as an example. My pastor had been the president of a university at a time they experienced a tragedy which prompted an appearance by Jesse Jackson (with all the media in tow). Yes, he had his photo-ops aplenty, but the Reverend explained that his ministry was "being there" – literally coming alongside people in pain and being there with them. Now, whether you appreciate Jesse Jackson or not, the concept is still important.

As a coach, you are constantly practicing the patience and diligence of just being there.

And when all else fails, do this: go to the joy. What does that mean? It means that when you can't seem to catch a break with your struggling teachers and you're just beaten up by negativity and push-back to your coaching, go and hang out with the teachers who are doing the right thing. Find joy in what's going right and leave what's going wrong aside for a few days.

Connecting Your Coaching to the Common Core

Before you take off at a million miles a minute and implement the Common Core Standards, consider this: are there topics, ideas or questions that we need to research before we implement?

I encourage you to pull your staff together and take ten minutes to brainstorm all of the questions that you have about the Common Core and then assign items on your list to each teacher team to research. Then at your next staff meeting, have the teams share their findings. I promise that your resistance and being overwhelmed about Common Core will decrease significantly because you have taken the time to arm your staff with information before they take action.

Coaching Through Those Sticky Situations

Facebook fan, Jennifer D. asks: *Jill, what are the top five things you should never say to a teacher while coaching, because it will backfire?*

Only five? Okay – you've issued me a good challenge here! Here are my "Top 5 Never Say to a Teacher You're Coaching Unless You Want a Door Slammed in Your Face" statements:

1. *"It's not my fault the district is making us do it."* This communicates a complete lack of conviction about what it is that you're coaching. A resistant teacher will glom onto this and never let it go.

2. *"When I was in my classroom, I…"* This is just really annoying. Come up with alternatives like, "You know, when I was in Mr. Thomas' classroom, I saw him doing _____ and I think that would work really well for you, too."

3. *"I don't know."* You've got a limited number of "I don't knows" in your coaching bank. Use them sparingly or else teachers will wonder how you can support them, since it seems like you know so little.

4. *"I'm so sorry that I didn't make our debriefing yesterday."* Make a commitment to your teachers and keep it. This is a big "loss of trust" area for many coaches – and it's totally avoidable.

5. The last one is putting anything in email, text, IM, DM, message board, Post-It, scratch paper or message in a bottle that could possibly be misconstrued. I see coaches fall into this all of the time! They leave a "Come and talk to me" Post-It message on the teachers' desk and that's somehow seen as directive, offensive or mean. Coaches, just avoid it! Talk to your teachers. That's where the relationship is built.

THE ONE CONVERSATION YOU PROBABLY DON'T WANT TO HAVE

Originally appeared on www.jackson-consulting.com,
May 20, 2013

I was working with a principal and coach recently and we were talking about moving through some pretty tough resistance they were facing. I did some modeling and scripting for them on how to have straight-forward conversations with some key staff members who were causing an unnecessary ruckus (by the way, there are times that call for a necessary ruckus…I should know!). We talked about how, as leaders, you owe it to the people doing the "right thing" to do some confronting (I hate the connotation of that word, but you catch my drift) of the people doing the "wrong thing."

I also told the principal and coach that I don't think that just because people are doing things differently than we might expect them to, that they're "wrong," but the results of these particular ruckus-causers were really very poor. Their students were struggling and something had to be done.

As we were talking and modeling and coaching each other through how to have these conversations, one of the principals turned to me and said, "Oh, I'm just not like you. I don't like confrontation." I laughed (I've heard this before) and said, "Are you saying that I like it?" And she said, "Well it seems like it!" We all laughed even more.

What I told her is this: "I get butterflies, stomach aches, moments of wanting to live in denial, and all of that other stuff when I have to talk with someone about following the plan, poor behavior, or anything else that might be deemed confrontational. The difference is this: I just do it anyway."

See that's the real deal in school improvement, classroom improvement, teaching improvement, score improvement or anything-else-improvement. We OWE IT TO THOSE WE SERVE (the kids) and the ONES WE WORK ALONGSIDE (our colleagues) to bring it every day. And we really owe it to them to take care of situations where it's not being brought every day. Catch my drift?

I am more than convinced that leadership in the classroom, school and district is about skill, for sure. But it's more about guts.

Guts equals success. Notice I didn't say guts equals perfection, because I know for sure that we don't have to be perfect to get the results in the classroom that we want. That's the good news!

Do you have guts? Let's put it to the test.

I would like you to pull out a Post-It note. (Yes, really do this...I promise it'll be worth it!)

I want you to jot down the FIRST name that comes to mind when you read this question: Who is the one person that is getting in the way of my teaching/leadership/coaching improvement and success?

Jot down the name.

Now on another sticky note, I want you to jot down (really quickly – don't think too hard – we're going for a gut check here) the answer to this: What three specific actions does that person engage in or display that are getting in the way?

Now look at your list. Cross off anything that is a feeling, a thought, an idea. Only leave actions on the list.

Now to the hard part…

I want you to make an appointment with that person for a time within the next week. Instead of saying, "Wanda, I'd like to make an appointment. We need to talk" (which always gives me a heart attack and makes me want to move…to Siberia), say something like, "Wanda, can I have 30 minutes of your time on Thursday at 3:30? I want to run some ideas by you as I'm getting in my right mind for the next school year."

When you sit down with Wanda, for example, start off by saying something like: "Wanda I need your help with something…" or "Wanda, I'm really trying to be more efficient this year." Put it on yourself. But at some point (do it quickly before you chicken out), you will need to add in there, "Would you help me improve by making sure that when we're in our team meetings, we stick to our agenda?" (If, for example, the off-topic talking by Wanda is inhibiting your team's work).

The bottom line is this: the instruction doesn't just happen in the classroom with the kids. Many times there are staff/team/colleague issues that we need to hash out so that we can improve the quality of our teaching – and to ensure that we're bringing the best to our kids each day.

You've got to have guts in order to improve your performance, and that of your kids.

Do you?

Step 6: Get a Plan

I believe that all good things in life come down to a checklist. I know that's not a romantic or deep thought, but if you're looking to get things done, you've got to have a plan. The same goes for coaching!

I encourage you to put one item a day on your "to do" list. I promise that if you take things one step at a time, the cumulative effect will be powerful.

Don't over think, just do. Right now is when you'll start to build your coaching plan. These simple steps will help you structure your time and get organized on the coaching tasks and activities that matter. Here is your final checklist for coaching success:

- Set a weekly appointment to meet with the principal and guard it with your life

- Ask your principal to remind staff that coaching is a required component of professional development and that everyone will be coached

- Ask your principal what is his instructional focus

- Ask your principal to reinforce that instructional focus during the next three staff meetings

- Brainstorm all of the technical teaching components that go into accomplishing the principal's instructional focus in each classroom (NOTE: these technical components are what you will 'measure' during your Phase Two of coaching)

- Ask your principal to tie her instructional focus to your coaching role during the next three staff meetings

- Create a brochure for your coaching practice and highlight all of the coaching options

- Explicitly explain and field questions about the coaching brochure during the next staff meeting

- Create a coaching binder with a tab for every teacher you will coach. This is where you will keep your coaching notes and data for each teacher

- Institute a coaching schedule or calendar for yourself where you detail the who/what/when/where of each coaching engagement for the week (NOTE: this is different from a coaching log because you will assign times to coaching in advance)

- Determine whether you will start your coaching with a Concerns Based Statement to gather information from the entire staff

- Identify the teachers who will need classroom management support and put them on your calendar first

- Start coaching with your most open and honest teachers and ask them for feedback during your coaching

- Ask a coaching colleague to observe you in 2-3 debriefings and give you feedback on how to improve your coaching practice

- Set up a coaching log to ensure that you are varying your coaching styles and tailoring your support to teacher need

- Identify classrooms that will serve as great "co-observation" sites, and talk with those teachers about opening up their classrooms for this type of coaching

- Schedule drop-in visits across departments or grade levels to check in on progress toward the instructional focus for the year - these will not require a debriefing, but give you a big picture sense of how implementation is going overall

- Prioritize your visits based upon the data – the more the kids are struggling, the more coaching that teacher needs

- Put a reminder in your calendar to check in with teachers a few times this year and gather information about how they think the coaching is going

- Look for additional opportunities for coaching training, specifically those that allow you to get feedback as you coach

As you read this book, I hope that you noticed the threads of gutsiness and straightforwardness in each chapter, script and resource. Once we tell teachers that they will be coached and what they will be coached on, then we need to get the show on the road. After all, simply having a coach doesn't mean that there is coaching happening.

So, let's end this book right where we started: *Coaching is the number one, most readily-available tool that has the real-life power to transform the quality of teaching and the impact of teaching on student performance.*

Coaching Resources

Sample Reading Coach Schedule, Week 1

Monday 1 Tuesday 2	Wednesday 3	Thursday 4	Friday 5
Winter Break	First day back to school Reading coach training *Differentiated Instruction* **8-3pm**	Update pacing schedule and assessment collection dates Plan for grade level meetings, Gr. 2-3, K Schedule coverage for Kindergarten demonstration lesson and debriefing Grade level meeting, Gr. 3 **11-11:40am** Discuss upcoming assessments, schedule individual meetings to review data Review coach training notes and plan small-group instruction demonstration lessons and observations	Grade level meeting, Gr. 2 **11-11:40am** Discuss fluency building activities, schedule individual meetings Meeting with Mr. Saunders, Gr. 2 (new teacher) **12-12:30pm** Discuss training plan, schedule demonstration lessons and observations Principal update, meeting **1-2pm** Email/Paperwork

Sample Reading Coach Schedule, Week 2

Monday 8	Tuesday 9	Wednesday 10	Thursday 11	Friday 12
Demonstration lesson Mr. Saunders, Gr. 2 **8:45-9:30am** Plan for grade level meetings, Gr. 1, 4-5 Debrief with Mr. Saunders **12-12:25pm** Prep for demonstration lessons on fluency building routines, Gr. 1 Grade level meeting, Gr. K **12:30-1:10pm** Review latest assessment data, plan new areas for small group time, set up individuals	Grade level meeting, Gr. 5 **11-11:40am** Discuss implementing small-group time, set up grade level demonstration lesson Conduct fluency building demonstration lesson, Gr. 1-Mr. Orozco's class **8:45-9:45am** Study Gr. 3 research project options Prep for Gr. K demonstration lesson on sound/spelling cards	Accompany Mr. Saunders on grade level classroom visits to observe phonics and fluency instruction **8-11:30am** Grade level planning, Gr. 3 Research project **2:30-3:30pm** Debrief with Gr. 1 **11:45am-12:30pm** *working lunch	Conduct Gr. K demonstration lesson on sound/spelling cards Grade level meeting, Gr. 1 **11-11:40am** Discuss fluency building activities, schedule individual meetings Debrief with Gr. K **1-1:40pm** Shadow coach Mr. Saunders-small group time instruction **10:15-11am**	Shadow coach Mr. Saunders-small group time instruction **10:15-11am** Grade level meeting, Gr. 4 **11-11:40am** Discuss implementing small-group time, set up grade level demonstration lesson Principal update meeting **1-2pm** Email, Paperwork

Sample Reading Coach Schedule, Week 3

Monday 15	Tuesday 16	Wednesday 17	Thursday 18	Friday 19
Martin Luther King, Jr. Holiday	Meet with Mrs. Bedrosian, Gr. 5 **8:30-9am** Meet with Mrs. Burke, Gr. K-1 9-9:45am Small-group time instruction observation, Gr. 3 **10-11am** Reading coach meeting **2-3pm** Collect progress monitoring assessment data	Small-group time instruction observation, Gr. 4 **9-10am** Submit requests for "Reading" field trips to district office, Gr. 3-5 Plan paraprofessional training, 1/24 Check-in meeting with Mr. Saunders **3-3:30pm**	Observe small-group time instruction, Gr. 1-2 **10-11:30am** Data analysis Meet with Mr. Bader, Gr. 4 **1-1:30pm** Meet with Ms. Swanson and Mr. Takumah, Gr. 1 **1:45-2:30pm**	Plan upcoming observation with Ms. Whitney, Gr. 3 **7:30-8am** Debrief with Gr. 3 **12-12:30pm** Debrief with Gr. 4 **2-2:30pm** Principal update (email) Email, Paperwork Prep for upcoming K-3 lessons

Sample Reading Coach Schedule, Week 4

Monday 22	Tuesday 23	Wednesday 24	Thursday 25	Friday 26
Observe and debrief Mrs. Bedrosian, Gr. 5 **8:30-10am** Data analysis **10:45-11:15am** Debrief with Gr. 2 **12-12:30pm** Observe small-group time instruction, Gr. K	Observe and debrief Ms. Burke, Gr. K-1 **8:40-10:15am** Demonstration lesson and debrief Mr. Bader, Gr. 4 **10:30-11:45am** Debrief with Gr. 3 **12-12:30pm** Data analysis	Paraprofessional training **9-12pm** Check-in meeting with Mr. Saunders **3-3:30pm** Data analysis	Observe Gr. 4-5 small-group time instruction **11-11:45am** Demonstration lesson, Ms. Swanson, Gr. 1 (Swanson and Takumah observing) **8:30-9:45am** Debrief with Swanson and Takumah **3-3:45pm** Prepare data report for coach meeting Prep for upcoming 4-5 lessons	Observe Gr. 4-5 small-group time instruction **11-11:45am** Observe Ms. Whitney **8:30-9:30am** Debrief with Gr. 4 **2-3pm** Principal update, meeting **1:30-2:30pm** (data analysis) Email, Paperwork Prepare data report for coach meeting

Sample Reading Coach Schedule, Week 5

Monday 29	Tuesday 30	Wednesday Feb. 1	Thursday Feb. 2	Friday Feb. 3
Mr. Saunders follow-up training	Reading coach meeting	Coach training,	Review coach training notes	Plan grade level meetings and staff training
12-2pm	**2-3pm**	*Developing grade Level Coaches*	Follow-up on teacher requests	
*working lunch	Study Gr. 2 and 4 research project options	**9-3pm**	Collaborative Grade level planning, Gr. 2 and 4: Joint research project	*"Becoming program experts"*
Debrief with Gr. 5	Follow-up paraprofessional training			Principal update (email)
2-3pm	**9-12am**		**3-3:45pm**	Staff meeting: share data analysis report
Debrief with Ms. Whitney			Follow-up meeting with principal	
3-3:30pm			(data analysis)	**2-3pm**
Prepare data report for coach meeting (cont.)				Email, Paperwork

Coaching Feedback Template

Coach: _____

Date: _____

	Yes	No	Notes for Debriefing the Coach
Coach creates a physical atmosphere of collaboration			
Coach asks teacher to reflect on lesson immediately			
Coach uses various questions to prompt reflection as necessary during the conversation			
Coach utilizes written lesson/curriculum as a tool to modify and correct teacher behavior			
Coach omits "I like"-type comments from coaching situation			
Coach models routine/procedure for teacher, if necessary			
Coach asks teacher to practice routine/procedure right then, if modeling has occurred			
Coaching exchange results in clear "next steps" for follow up			
Coach completes coaching exchange by prompting reflection on the coaching process			

Additional Notes for Debriefing:

Sample Coaching Tracking Template/Log for Coaches

Focus Area: Practice and Application							
Provides hands-on materials for students to practice using new content knowledge / Uses activities that integrate all language skills (i.e.: reading, writing, listening & speaking)							
Teacher	Date Pre-Conference	Focus for Coaching	Date Coached and Method of Coaching	Date Debriefed	Next Steps	Next Date	Notes
Jonny Johnson	9-12-12	Materials management by the students and teacher	9-14-12 Observation	9-14-12	Set expectations for materials management so that materials do not become a distraction Design opportunities for students to explain how they used the manipulatives to learn the new concept -- put it in their own words	9-19-12	Send reminder via email to get a time for us to get together to plan lesson for demo on 9-19-12

Coaching Cycle Long-Term Log

Teacher: _____

Coach: _____

Dates: _____

Cycle 1		
Pre-Conference	*Collecting Data*	*Prompting Reflection*
Areas of Concern	What the data shows	Questions and Suggested Action
Area of Focus	I observed students…	Model New Technique(s)
Type of Coaching • side-by side • coach demo • coach observation of teacher • shadow teach • collaboratively observe another teacher • data study session	I observed the teacher…	Next Steps

The Anatomy of a Debriefing

1	Re-state the purpose of the obser-vation and what you were looking for	
2	Ask the teacher to reflect: *What did you want me to see while I was in the classroom? What had you wanted me to see or pick up during your lesson? What did it look like when the students were engaging in XYZ task? How did the student performance match/ not match your expectations?*	
3	Using your notes to begin, explain to the teacher what you saw, giv-ing the data	
4	Provide specific "Yes!" and spe-cific "I would like you to work on" statements, paying close attention to why you have these highlighted	Yes!: To work on:
5	Ask the teacher to reflect on your notes and employ the coach as necessary	
6	Choose a "next step" time to see changes implemented	

The Anatomy of a Debriefing - Sample

1	Re-state the purpose of the observation and what you were looking for	Hi Will! I'm so excited to meet with you to discuss your lesson yesterday. Remember that during our pre-conference we decided that it would be important to get some feedback on the number of student responses that you get when you ask the whole class to take an action. The example you gave me is that, when you ask your students to use their note sheet to jot down two ideas from the text they've read, you're noticing only about 50 percent of your kids actually do that. So, I set out during my observation to gather some information on that for you.
2	Ask the teacher to reflect	So Will, tell me what you thought about the level of engagement during the time I was in there. What did you notice? If you had a chance to do this lesson again, would you change anything? What might you adjust for tomorrow's lesson, based upon the students' performance today?
3	Using your notes to begin, explain to the teacher what you saw, giving the data	Will, I counted that there were seven times in 15 minutes that you asked students to jot down "one thing they learned" during the minutes of reading and prior instruction. You gave an average wait time of 15 seconds before you asked students to write. Five of your seven jot downs lasted 20 seconds and two took about 35 seconds. Once you redirected the students to wait until they had their think-time, I noticed that 100 percent of the students were jotting down their notes when you prompted them.
4	Provide specific "Yes!" and specific "I would like you to work on" statements, paying close attention to why you have these highlighted	Yes! Will, this was a huge improvement from your last engagement level during your jotting down period. You went from about 50 percent of your kids jotting down notes to nearly 100 percent! That was fantastic to watch! I also noted that you had no blurting of answers during this time and you didn't have to make one redirection for behaviors. EXCELLENT JOB! Did you notice a difference?
		To work on:
		The one thing that I would like for you to consider is having students extend their responses. As I looked on during their note-taking, I realized that all of the students were writing very simple, five- or six-word sentences. You and I both know that your kids can do more! Since you have done such a nice job of getting the engagement levels up, I'd like for you to work on improving the quality of their responses by starting with asking them to at least write compound sentences. I think they'll be much better set up for their writing later in the day.
5	Ask the teacher to reflect on your notes and employ the coach as necessary	What do you think?
6	Choose a "next step" time to see changes implemented	Okay, so let's jot down on this Post-It right now what you'll try and then a date and time when I can get back into your classroom and see how things are going.

Coaching Prompts and Starters

- Tell me how you're structuring your time as you teach XYZ

- What lessons are you presenting?

- What components are you implementing to the intensive/strategic/benchmark students? How is that going?

- What parts of the lesson are a "slam dunk" and which leave you feeling less than accomplished?

- I know that we focused on XYZ previously. How is your continued implementation of those techniques going? What areas can use further refining just like we did with XYZ?

- I know that you were focused on bringing Johnny, Juan and Emelinda to benchmark. How is their progress? What have you tried? In what areas do you need further support?

- Tell me a little more about…

- Let me see if I understand…

- I'm wondering…

- I talked with Mrs. Jones about XYZ yesterday. How are you feeling about that area?

Debriefing Prompts and Reflection Kick-Starts

- *How did you think the lesson went?*

- *What would you do differently? Why?*

- *What triggered that thought?*

- *How is this different from how you might have delivered the lesson?*

- *Tell me what you thought when…*

- *How do you know that…?*

- *What I hear you saying is…*

- *What were you surprised about?*

- *What can you imagine us focusing on next?*

- *This leads me to think that we should take a look at…*

Team Meeting Record Sheet: Grade _____

Date: _____

Start Time: _____

End Time: _____

Attendees:

_____ _____ _____

_____ _____ _____

Facilitator: _____

Scribe: _____

Timekeeper: _____

Review expected outcomes for the meeting

1.

2.

3.

Topic #1

Define the issue/concern/problem:

What data supports this issue? What data do we need?

Generating Options:

Specific Team Actions

Action	Who?	By When?	Check in Date?

Individual Teacher Conference Record Sheet

Teacher: _____   Grade: _____

Coach: _____   Date: _____

How it's going:
Items discussed:
For future discussions:

Teacher Action Steps	Coach Action Steps	Other Action Steps

Next Meeting? What to bring to the meeting?

CPSIA information can be obtained
at www.ICGtesting.com
Printed in the USA
BVOW11s0515050817
491157BV00007B/135/P